MW00378813

Upstairs at the Roosevelts'

Growing Up with Franklin and Eleanor

CURTIS ROOSEVELT

Potomac Books

AN IMPRINT OF THE UNIVERSITY OF NEBRASKA PRESS

© 2017 by the estate of Curtis Roosevelt

All photos courtesy of Curtis Roosevelt

All rights reserved. Potomac Books is an imprint of
the University of Nebraska Press.
Manufactured in the United States of America.
∞

Library of Congress Cataloging-in-Publication Data
Names: Roosevelt, Curtis, 1930–2016, author.
Title: Upstairs at the Roosevelts': growing up with
Franklin and Eleanor / Curtis Roosevelt.
Description: Lincoln: Potomac Books, an imprint of
the University of Nebraska Press, 2017. | Includes
bibliographical references.
Identifiers: LCCN 2016047606
ISBN 9781612349015 (cloth: alk. paper)
ISBN 9781612349404 (epub)
ISBN 9781612349411 (mobi)
ISBN 9781612349428 (pdf)
Subjects: LCSH: Roosevelt, Curtis, 1930–2016—
Childhood and youth. | Roosevelt, Franklin D.
(Franklin Delano), 1882–1945—Family. | Roosevelt,
Eleanor, 1884–1962—Family. | Grandchildren of
presidents—United States—Biography. | Presidents—
United States—Family. | Presidents—United
States—Biography. | Presidents' spouses—United
States—Biography.
Classification: LCC E807.1.R48 R65 2017 | DDC
973.917092/2—dc23 LC record available at https://
lccn.loc.gov/2016047606

Set in Iowan Old Style by Rachel Gould.

To my dear wife, Marina

CONTENTS

ILLUSTRATIONS

INTRODUCTION

Because my sister and I often lived with these close relatives, I came to know my Roosevelt grandparents, Franklin and Eleanor, well. Indeed we lived in the White House for many years as youngsters, and as teenagers as well, and also at the family's home at Hyde Park. One forgets that FDR was elected four times as president, and Springwood at Hyde Park—the Big House, as the family referred to it—was my grandfather's home, in which he was born and to which he often returned, if only for a long weekend. Leaving Washington late in the evening, he could be home by early the next morning.

These chapters, only a few of the many that form my recollections, are my memories. So of course they are opinionated. My sister might well have different views. But I believe I am a better observer than she is. And I know I have a better memory!

The chapters cover a lot of ground, and much of it has been written about by FDR's biographers. I have the advantage of actually having been present in the scenes I describe. And indeed I am opinionated.

What you will read here has been written over the past ten years, although I have had trouble applying myself to the task in the past couple of years. Had it not been for the encouragement of my editor, Sarah Harrison, I do wonder if I would ever have completed them. Life in my mid-eighties does slow me down!

UPSTAIRS AT THE ROOSEVELTS'

1

My Twelve Years in the White House

The question most frequently asked of me is, "What was life like in the White House?" A response saying that it was "wonderful, fantastic, unforgettable and yet a disaster" only provokes a host of other questions. Until I wrote my book *Too Close to the Sun: Growing Up in the Shadow of My Grandparents, Franklin and Eleanor*, I hadn't thought too closely about this extraordinary experience of mine. But then I had to buckle down and think it through. I did, and a lot of illusions went out the window.

Twelve years is a long time in the life of a child.

In 1933 I was a toddler, three years old, when we went to live in the White House. By 1945, when my grandfather, President Roosevelt, died, I was just fifteen. The White House had proved a steady series of events, punctuated by an equally steady stream of visitors. During those twelve years, circulating within that hothouse of bustling politics, I met a lot of people. By the age of fifteen, I had met everybody from Winston Churchill to Mary Martin!

I listened and absorbed, especially when I was old enough, at age nine, to be included with the adults at mealtimes. It was my education—far more important than any formal one I have had. By fifteen I was quite sophisticated politically. I could converse easily with the many guests at the dining table. But usually I was "seen and not heard," as was considered courteous and proper for my age. Knowing your place was a dictum drummed into me from early childhood.

When doing the research for my book—which included a lot of dredging through my exciting and often difficult memories—I realized the extent to which I had been shaped by my years in the White House and by being President and Mrs. Roosevelt's eldest grandson, and it is a "shaping" that has continued throughout my life. It is in fact a distortion compared to a more normal upbringing. It is difficult to explain except in broad terms.

Power is very attractive. Everyone is to some degree drawn to it, but when you live within the walls of a place like the White House, it matters hugely, especially if you are a youngster. And, as I have noted, when everyone singles you out as an exception because of being the president and first lady's grandson, it is or becomes your identity, a part of who you are. When I first went to a public school and was introduced to my second-grade classmates, my teacher announced, "This is Buzzie. He has been living with his grandparents, the president and Mrs. Roosevelt, in the White House." The relationship with my future classmates was thus marked.

Buzzie (either with a *y* or an *ie*) was my nickname. Eleanor, my older sister, was known as Sistie. In 1933, in the midst of the Great Depression, the press picked up on these two little darlings living in the White House and had a grand time with us. Sistie-and-Buzzie became one word. We were featured in newspapers, magazines, and newsreels all over the country. Complicating that exposure for me was my grandmother and mother's dictum that we "do not like" having our picture taken; we do not like publicity! My sister echoed them and a barb could be thrust at me, "Buzzie *likes* having his picture taken!" I ducked my head and tried to adjust to this contradictory party line. But of course I enjoyed the fuss; and most young boys might feel the same. Nonetheless, it brought conflict for me.

I liked the attention given me by the White House butlers and maids, as well as the Secret Service men guarding my grandfather. I was a kind of mascot. I enjoyed being included in pictures with my grandfather or grandmother. I loved being a part of their entourage. Living in the White House as we did, many opportunities daily presented themselves for being recognized. Even when Sis and I traveled on the train to New York, on our way from Washington to Hyde Park, we would be pointed at, "There's Sistie-and-Buzzie!" As if we were a single entity. My sister would duck her head; I'd look up and smile, enjoying the recognition. Our nurse then would hurry us on to the waiting Secret Service car.

But all this, and especially the conflict presented by my mother and grandmother, was not the best way for a child to grow up and mature. Indeed, life in the White House gave me a very complicated sense of identity, one that took years to work out of. "Watch your step!" was my byword.

My memories of those early days in the White House are filled with many activities, mainly with me as an observer. I liked parades, especially of soldiers and sailors. The marines had the best uniforms, I would pronounce, but quickly shut up when I saw that my keen interest was not conforming to the expected modesty at which my sister excelled. Still, my enthusiasm could not always be contained. I liked living in the White House, even though, as my mother frequently declared, "It's not good for Buzzie!"

As a small child, I found our daily routine to be marvelous. Every morning my sister and I would be brought to our grandfather's bedroom. We would burst in, completely unaware that we were interrupting his morning staff meeting. Papa, as we called our grandfather, would be propped up on pillows in his bed and was very welcoming. Up we would jump and roughhouse for a bit. "What are you going to do today?" would be the usual question. FDR was a wonderful grandfather, but soon, within five minutes, the work of the president of the United States had to continue. So we then would be whisked out by our waiting nurse.

A visit to our grandmother was much more subdued, more regulated, with my sister answering most questions. When with our mother, her attention was focused on our nurse who was instructed about where we should be, and at what time, what we should wear, and any other practical details that seemed necessary. Each day usually had an event that requiring Sis and me to be prepared. But my sister would opt out of standing in receiving lines where my grandmother would be shaking hands with several hundred people. I liked the recognition—"This is Buzzie," I'd be introduced—then correctly extending my hand to be shook. Even at age five I considered this as part of the game, one at which I was soon adept.

When I was seven, we moved from the White House to a new home in Seattle. Leaving it was painful, and I mourned not being daily in that atmosphere I'd so thrilled to. Life in the White House had been a mixture of the wonderful and the disastrous. However, I wouldn't fully grasp the latter until I reached midlife.

My memories are richly filled with those days in the White House. It was marvelous, a lark, brimming with unique experiences, ones I will never forget.

2

Hyde Park, Our Family Home

When I grew up on my family's estate at Hyde Park in the 1930s, I had no idea how passé, how archaic, such a lifestyle was. It was practically out of a Victorian or Edwardian play or film. But it was all that I knew, and it was my world. The nursery on the third floor of the Big House formed my earliest memories. Throughout my childhood and youth, I did not really comprehend that life under my great-grandmother's tutelage was totally out of date. It was the end of an era and had been on its way out since before the First World War. Sara Delano Roosevelt's death in 1941 was one of the events marking its demise as a way of life that had defined the landscape of the private lives of America's wealthy upper class.

In 1935–36 when the Vanderbilt estate, a mile up the Hudson River from our more modest place, came on the block, probably to be broken up into smaller plots, my grandfather, Franklin Delano Roosevelt, asked the Interior Department to purchase it as a national historic site. Behind his request was his notion that the American people should visit and see for themselves how a wealthy few of our countrymen had lived in the Gilded Age, before federal income tax existed. The Vanderbilt estate now is managed by the U.S. National Park Service, the other two in the immediate area being my family's estate, Springwood, and my grand-mother's house, Val-Kill.

Although the Park Service guides do not mention my grand-father's rationale for preserving the Vanderbilt estate as a public site when interpreting to visitors the house where I grew up—Springwood—Franklin Roosevelt might also have been commenting on his own home. Just like the Vander-bilt estate, the Big House, with its large stables and carriage house—later the garage—laundry house, icehouses, exten-sive "greenhouse," superintendent's cottage and numerous servants' quarters, would be impossible to maintain privately after World War II. Not only was it hugely expensive but, practically speaking, there was no more of the cheap labor that once had made it all possible. With very few excep-tions, such big estates are now only useful for conversion into schools, clinics, old-age homes, and historic sites. Yet thank God we have them. It is through visiting them that a part of our history, our heritage, can come alive.

So I begin with my memories, ones located, of course, in the same nursery my grandfather occupied, as had my mother and all my uncles, and my sister, too, I expect. It is a large room, with a crib in one corner and another bed oppo-site for the nurse. Windows on three sides give great light as well as provide breezes on the hot sultry nights of sum-mer. Double doors lead to the large area over the big library on the first floor.

When it became light I awoke. Through the slats of my crib I could see Beebee's bed.[1] It was comforting to have her close by; I could hear her gentle snoring during the night.

But the bed was empty. I wasn't disturbed; I knew the routine. Beebee had left to dress herself in one of the white starched uniforms she always wore. She would return. And when she did I was lifted out of my crib, taken into the bathroom, cleaned up, and then dressed in a shirt and pin-afore—my own regular uniform.

Back in the nursery I was placed in a small chair that

matched the small round table in front of me to await my breakfast. It arrived on a tray, brought by the number-two butler from the kitchen on the first floor. It remained warm due to the hot water underneath the three receptacles for food on my plate—obviously designed for a long journey such as the one from kitchen to nursery. There might be a piece of fresh fruit, and always there was the silver cup with my milk. My godmother had given me that cup upon my christening ceremony and I still have it, quite dented from those earlier days.

After breakfast it was out of the house to the stables, running and shouting all the way. We were on schedule, roughly 9:30, and Sgt. George Carnahan and Corporal "Slim" had the horses ready. Sis had the spunkier one, Natoma, my mother's Arabian. I had my grandmother's quieter mare, Dot, which her friend Earl Miller had given her and on which Grandmère, my grandmother Eleanor, had won several blue ribbons at horse shows. I was proud of riding Dot. I was no longer on a lead rope, but Slim kept a close eye on me. Though even Dot had run away with me the previous summer and once I had fallen off—I can't say "thrown" as I just rolled off, due to not gripping sufficiently with my knees. I was lazy and never bothered to ride properly in an English saddle. But I did love to look around—I was content to walk and didn't mind if Sis and Sgt. George trotted or cantered ahead. Slim was easy about this except to remind me that we did have to trot now and then to catch up with Sis if we were going to see which path they next took. I loved old Dot. Grandmère, who would only occasionally ride Dot, wrote to my mother that I now considered Dot "my horse."

Sis didn't like waiting for me at the next turn. Which path to take, which route to go, was dictated by my sister—she was in the lead—and she delighted in choosing a direction challenging for me. I didn't mind, I liked riding through the woods and on the sides of the fields, letting Dot take her own sweet time. That we might return to the stable ten minutes behind Sis and George didn't bother me. We usually were out for about an hour and a half. If time permitted we might feed the horses a carrot or a bit of grain from the palm of our hand. Keep the palm of your hand flat, we were instructed, for horses have big teeth.

But before noon we were due in the house to wash off the smell of horse and stable before eating. If we were to lunch with my great-grandmother, Sara, washing meant having a quick bath.

In the summer afternoons, after my nap, Sis and I would return to the stables where George and Slim had hitched up Natoma to one of the remaining family carriages. It was a buggy, with two persons in front and two squeezed into a smaller back seat. As Beebee had done, Duffie (Elizabeth McDuffie, one of our maids and the wife of my grandfather's valet) liked to accompany us on our buggy ride. She and I sat in back. Sis was in front with Sgt. Carnahan, who firmly held the reins and moved Natoma into a trot as long as the road was gravel. On dirt paths with their many ruts and potholes from the rain, Natoma walked peacefully under the trees. Occasionally Sis was allowed to hold the reins. A drive in a horse-drawn carriage—your family's carriage—is an experience long gone. (The Central Park buggies for the New York tourists aren't the same thing.)

As usual we passed the Newbolds' next door, meandered past the Rogers' home, and then on to the Vanderbilt estate. The huge trees on their property were, and remain, exceptional. They had been planted in the eighteenth century by the Bard family. The Bards' classic colonial mansion wasn't quite big enough—or grand enough—for the Vanderbilts, so they tore it down and erected a blown-up version of the Petit Trianon at the Versailles Palace, just outside Paris. The result is a bloated building that has lost its original lovely proportions. (For me it resembles a typical public library, in the style of those donated by Andrew Carnegie around the country.) But the Vanderbilts did not alter the landscaping with its carefully selected trees brought from different parts of the world.

With George holding the reins we might carefully cross the busy Albany Post Road to explore the fantastic complex of buildings the Vanderbilts had erected for their horses and carriages and to store their hay. It was in disrepair even when I saw it as a young child in the late thirties, but, still, its block-square cobblestone courtyard, symmetrically arranged buildings on three sides, the huge barn at the end, and the grand well in the center of the courtyard made for an enviable scene. Then heading back across Route 9, we would return the few miles to the Big House by a different route, all at our same leisurely pace. Going home to her stall and a bag of oats, Natoma trotted easily the last half-mile.

Sometimes during our carriage rides a thunderstorm would appear in the sky and George would whip up Natoma to get home, before the rain came pouring down and the thunder cracked. There was always the possibility that this might have sent Natoma rearing and perhaps bolting. I saw it as much fun and excitement—if only the conjuring up of potential danger. But most often we trotted rapidly home without mishap, leaving Natoma barely sweating.

The organization within the Big House, as well as its atmosphere, was very Anglophilic, much like the other estates along the Hudson River. Even before Sara had married the widowed James Roosevelt, he had been nicknamed "the Squire" because of his "pork-chop" beard, then very stylish in England. The Roosevelts journeyed once a year to Europe, spending time in Britain, France, the Low Countries, Germany, Austria, and Italy. Both my great-grandfather (whom I never knew) and my great-grandmother, "Granny," were reasonably fluent in other languages, particularly French and German. But it was through their British friends that they took their cues for the lifestyle at their own estate in America.

But in no way did I feel England to be "the mother country." I understood it simply to be the one where household standards were set. The butler, the cook, and the succession of nannies and tutors we had often were hired through London agencies. Granny normally had six or eight "inside" servants and six "outside" servants, supplemented by more when guests would arrive to stay or family would come to spend vacations.

Because travel in the nineteenth century was arduous and time consuming, guests typically stayed at Hyde Park for several days, even a couple of weeks. They expected to be looked after in the manner to which they were accustomed, so servants were very important on that scene, indeed essential. Without servants, not only the work but the whole social structure would have fallen apart. What would the "upstairs" be without the "downstairs"? And, of course there would have been no "downstairs" without an "upstairs" to serve. It was a lifestyle that doesn't exist anymore because people are not willing to fit into it. Such a lifestyle flowed directly from an accepted class society and labor being cheap. No longer—not in affluent Western countries anyway. Even well into the twentieth century, going "into service" was often a step up for many people, but to succeed they had to quickly adopt the expected manners of the Big House.

Life changed substantially in the Big House when Granny departed for her annual summer month on the island of Campobello in New Brunswick's Bay of Fundy. The butler returned to England for his holiday. So did the cook. Jennings, Granny's maid, went along with her. Except for Jennings, Granny always "made do" at Campo with a locally recruited staff put together by the resident housekeeper, Mrs. Calder.

Was my great-grandmother roughing it at Campobello? Well, yes, but back in New York, so were we! In the Big House we were left with only the number-two butler, someone local brought in to do the cooking, and no more than one person coming in during the day to clean. Mrs. Depew still did the laundry, which didn't amount to much. And there was, of course, our nurse. The Big House seemed empty. The routine was the same—except that we might have tea on the back porch with the servants. But there was no Granny at the center of it all. We didn't even go to church in the village except if Grandmère was visiting her place, Val-Kill, and took us with her.

To some extent, after Granny departed, Grandmère stepped in to supervise Sis and me. We went to Val-Kill at least once a day. After our morning spent riding we quite often went there for lunch. Being about two miles east from the Big House it took about fifteen minutes by car. The quickest way was on a small dirt road winding through the woods.

Things were more casual at Val-Kill. We might even have hamburgers or hot dogs grilled on Grandmère's barbeque, which looked like a big fireplace set on the lawn. Everyone joined in—she always had guests—with the cooking and serving. My grandmother, of course, did not know how to cook, although she was quite willing to turn over a hamburger if someone told her when to do it. She had servants in the kitchen to prepare food, serve, and do the household chores. But, compared to the regime in the Big House, Grandmère's household help were relaxed in their approach to their jobs. (Grandmère once hired the brother of Josh White, the well-known folk singer, to be her butler and chauffeur. Although William had never done anything like that before, he needed a job, Grandmère rationalized. Granny's English butler would have been horrified watching William who, with his very long arms, removed a soiled plate from the left and served a clean one from the right all in one swift movement.)

Grandmère shared the swimming pool at Val-Kill with Nancy Cook and Marion Dickerman. She had been close friends with them during the 1920s and early thirties. Whenever she had had a free day or two she came to Val-Kill and shared the house, known as the Stone Cottage, with Marion and Nancy. Eleanor considered it her home, a place to retreat from the Big House. Shortly after my grandmother became first lady, and began to play an influential role in American life across the country, others entered her life—like Lorena Hickok, or "Hick," with whom she was close—people that Marion and Nancy didn't like. Grandmère then decided to build her own house by putting together two of the Val-Kill furniture buildings nearby. (The Val-Kill furniture enterprise, begun in 1926, had gone, unfortunately, down the tubes, with my grandmother having to buy a good deal of the furniture.)

By 1937, when Sis and I returned to Hyde Park after living in Seattle for six months, the relationship among the three women had cooled. The tension was obvious. Our mother had briefed us on what to expect. We were not supposed to notice the estrangement, but we could see plainly that Grandmère now had a place to herself. We still referred to Grandmère's friends as Aunt Marion and Aunt Nancy, and they were still invited to the Big House for a meal whenever FDR was visiting.

Grandmère's own house at Val-Kill had only recently been finished. According to biographer Joseph Lash, she felt, she said, that for the first time in her life she really had a home of her own. The pine paneling throughout had a pleasant rustic feel, but the rooms were furnished just as my grandmother always furnished her houses, in a simple, homey good taste, with bookcases and pictures, mostly family and friends, covering the walls.

In recognition of Eleanor's dependence upon Malvina "Tommy" Thompson, her resident secretary—who was on call at any hour of the day or evening that my grandmother might be want to work—Tommy had her own apartment, joining Grandmère's house through a doorway. There she had her own living room with a large screened porch, a kitchen, her own bedroom, and guest room. Traditionally, family and guests always gathered in "Tommy's room," her living room and office, for cocktails, using her kitchen as a bar. Also, Grandmère freely filled Tommy's guest room with her own guests, but only after dutifully checking that Tommy's friend Henry Osthagen was not arriving for the weekend. And, probably most annoying to Tommy, we regularly passed through her sitting room and office, using it as the passageway into Grandmère's house.

Actually, Tommy never seemed bothered by our regular intrusions of one sort or another into her space. Some of Grandmère's guests annoyed her but her reaction to them had nothing to do with their trespassing. As for us kids, the few of us who spent a lot of time at Val-Kill, Tommy was our second grandmother, and it seemed more natural, and easier, to interrupt her rather than to bother Grandmère.

The one exception to these interruptions was a daily occurrence when quiet was expected. Grandmère was "doing her column." Eleanor would draw up a chair to Tommy's desk and dictate her My Day column—which ran in newspapers across the country—directly to Tommy. As Tommy didn't know shorthand, she took this dictation directly onto the typewriter. Having never been through a proper typing course, she typed with two or three fingers of each hand—very rapidly. Sometimes I felt Grandmère's columns were excellent, especially when she felt particularly strongly about a subject. But they could also read as if she had written them right off the top of her head and hadn't had very much to say that day.

A small staircase led to the second floor of Val-Kill. At the end of a narrow hallway was Grandmère's modestly sized bedroom with its large screened sleeping porch attached. Right before this were two small guest rooms—only one was large enough for two beds, just barely. Other guest bedrooms were over Tommy's apartment. Bathrooms in the house were small, very utilitarian.

While lacking any grandeur, the whole place had a character that reflected the warmth of my grandmother, as a person, as a hostess. While the house still showed the class background of her childhood, Val-Kill expressed Eleanor's rebellion against the nineteenth-century atmosphere of Springwood and the class distinctions it reflected, ones that came so naturally to her mother-in-law.

Val-Kill was also my grandmother's way of establishing her own style, one she felt was more in tune with the way the world was developing, in keeping with a more egalitarian society. But just as in the White House, or in her own apartment in New York, Grandmère maintained the old tradition of covering the walls with pictures of family and friends. Too, family silver defined her Val-Kill dining room. She kept teatime, with all the trimmings, serving everyone herself—just as she did in the White House. Val-Kill had a distinct atmosphere, casual and friendly, welcoming visitors with the look of cluttered living space fully occupied that my grandmother would have been accustomed to since childhood.

In the way that the Big House and the Hyde Park estate was centered on Sara, Val-Kill always revolved around Eleanor.

Eleanor Roosevelt enjoyed company; indeed, she didn't like being alone. Every weekend she filled the house with guests, and, if she wasn't traveling, she was never without company even during the week. Grandmère's schedule kept her in New York City and on the road during the winter months, so she was rarely at Val-Kill for more than a few days at a time. But when spring moved into summer, she would try to be present more frequently. This was so especially if Sis and I were staying at the Big House—and Granny wasn't around, either abroad or having gone to Campobello.

The screened porch off my grandmother's bedroom was where she slept at Val-Kill during the warm and humid summer nights. Grandmère loved being "outside." She had the largest daybed I'd ever seen. It had been made to order at Val-Kill for my six-foot-five-inch uncle, John Roosevelt, who never used it. So my grandmother took it back. I would take my afternoon naps on it, occupying about one-third of its length.

I often went swimming with Sis in the pool at Stone Cottage. I paddled about in the shallow end. Sis could swim pretty well and had just learned to dive off the side of the pool. My special delight was holding on to the pool's edge where the water gushed out, keeping the pool water circulating. It was of such force that it nearly swept me off.

Some guests might also be swimming in the pool, but I was scared of the many offers I had to teach me how to swim "all the way to the deep end." My grandmother's former bodyguard, Earl Miller—a New York State trooper who'd become her good friend—was the only one able to give me confidence. By the end of the summer I could make it to the end of the pool, although still only dog paddling. My "coach" said the most important thing was for me to know that I could get to the other end of the pool. Later I learned it was he who had also given my grandmother the confidence to swim well, to start riding horseback again, and to recommence driving a car.

Sis and I had known Sergeant Miller ever since his assignment as my grandmother's bodyguard. He had been one of the state troopers assigned to them when FDR was governor of New York State. In time he became part of the extended family that included Aunt Marion, Aunt Nancy, Hick, Marguerite "Missy" LeHand, Tommy, Louis Howe, and Gus Gennerich, Papa's bodyguard. They had their meals with us. Granny probably raised her eyebrows at having Earl and Gus "at table," but that's what Grandmère and Papa wanted, hence the two were included. My great-grandmother's ambivalence was apparent to Sis and me. We didn't really know how to address them; nobody encouraged us to call them "Uncle Earl" or Uncle Gus."

Louis Howe was, of course, among those at the table. Although part of the extended family for long before either of us was born, he was always "Mr. Howe" to Sis and me. To this day I can smell the Sweet Caporal cigarettes he regularly smoked. They were pungent. The ashes from his cigarettes fell down the front of whatever he was wearing. Granny said he was "dirty." And so he was, relatively speaking, but his overall effect was one I found distinctive, different from the others in our extended family. Indeed, Mr. Howe often smelled rather stale, but my grandfather never seemed to object. Louis Howe was his ally, without a doubt the most important person in helping FDR achieve his ambition of being president. I could sense his and my grandfather's mutual rapport.

In the late afternoons at Val-Kill, Grandmère would walk over for her swim, a bathrobe worn over her suit. Her daily swim was a routine, a self-imposed discipline—for exercise, she said. And that was the way she approached it. Standing on the side of the pool, pumping her legs, she got off the edge with a low dive. It was always a belly flop. And if any of my uncles were around, hoots and derisive remarks—akin to schoolboy teasing—inevitably followed. Grandmère took two turns each length, one a breast stroke and the other a side stroke.[2] Afterward, she got out and lay down by the side of the pool to sun herself for a few minutes.

Swimming might be followed by tea at the poolside. It was usually iced tea with fresh mint from the garden accompanied by cake and cookies. Although Val-Kill was informal, Sis and I never helped ourselves without permission. Manners were maintained, even if you were wearing only a bathing suit.

When we arrived at Hyde Park it always seemed an endless period stretching ahead. That we'd have to leave didn't occur to me. But the time slipped past. Early in 1937, my mother, my sister, my mother's second husband (John Boettiger), and I had moved out of the White House and across the country to Seattle. That summer Grandmère would announced that Sis and I would shortly have to leave for Seattle to resume our schools. We would, however, wait for Granny to return from Campobello, as she insisted upon seeing us again. But then it was the train for New York where we would meet Mademoiselle Deschamps, our governess. She would accompany us on the long train ride across the country.

I felt like a balloon with its air released, flattened. Duffie comforted me. She reminded me that I would soon be seeing my mother and stepfather. That did not bring relief. The thought of losing Duffie's company mattered more. I felt at home in the Big House, and with Granny, and with everyone else at Hyde Park. I liked being at Val-Kill with Grandmère and Tommy. And now I was being sent back to a life away from all of this. The old feeling of being sent into exile from home returned.

In the summer holidays we returned at last to Hyde Park. Home again! I would be back in my old bed in the nursery, with Sis back in "her" room, our mother's childhood room. Duffie was nearby, installed in one of the two rooms for the children's nurses on the stairwell landing. Lying in my bed, the memories flooded back. My old crib rested on the other side of the room. Slowly the memory returned to me of Beebee when she had slept across from me, but she was gone now and I put it out of my mind. The same little table and matching chairs for my meals were in the middle of the room. When I was an infant I had taken all my meals there, before my table manners were thought sufficiently well developed to eat with my older sister in the dining room.

Now Sis and I usually ate our meals in the little alcove off the dining room, quite the best place with its bay window and view over the Hudson. Breakfasts at the Big House are a valued memory. My mother and uncles always waxed nostalgic when remembering them, especially the fresh butter, cream so thick, as they used to say, that you couldn't even pour it, and milk unpasteurized—and yes, it does taste different than today's homogenized milk. The honey and marmalade were special, I was told. There were bacon and eggs and brown toast to go with it.

Sis and I would talk of what we were going to do that day, although, when I think about it, the options were few. We were back in the old routine. The only change was that, now being a year older, I could stay up a little longer in the evening, maybe a half-hour. The day's schedule was completely occupying, quite exhausting, and that was the way we expected it. The notion of having fun or not having fun didn't occur to us. I couldn't imagine, and still can't, doing anything better than the day's routine. Life was full, and fun.

At night there would be the usual sound of the train traveling alongside the Hudson River, pulling slowly up the grade on its way to Albany, and then on to the West. And the thunderstorms at night could be fierce, providing much to talk about at breakfast. But most of all, the feeling of coming home was the familiarity of people, the rooms in the Big House, their furniture and the smell of polish, the laundry room with its particular smell, the stable, carriage house, the greenhouse, the ice house, the lawn and big trees in the spacious grounds, the vegetable garden. All familiar. I belonged.

There was for me, as well, enormous security with Granny. It was her place, the Big House and the surrounding estate. I identified with it, and with her. I felt at home with Granny. I did not doubt her authority—and she could be quite formidable. But that didn't matter, as I felt her unreserved love.

When lunching with Granny at Hyde Park, particularly after a long morning of horseback riding, it was essential that Duffie clean us up and make us presentable. If Granny had a guest, it was usually a family member. Lunch at the big table was served by both butlers. The guest was served first, then Granny, then Sis, and then me. We began with a soup served from a tureen and ladled by the butler into my bowl. The large spoon on the right-hand side of the place setting was quite heavy—using it required close attention if I wasn't to spill any soup.

Next came a meat course. Again, the flatware was large. By this era I was being expected to cut my own meat, and do it smartly. The vegetables might be a separate course, especially if it was corn on the cob. That could be eaten in one's fingers. (But don't gobble!) Then salad followed.

Before dessert the butler set down in front of you a finger bowl with your dessert plate underneath. I learned to dip just so much of my fingers into the bowl—"not to take a bath"—before carefully picking up the bowl, *and* its doily underneath, and removing them up and to the left, where my bread plate had been before it had been removed. It seemed to me an unnecessary addition to eating a meal, yet it added a formality, a distinction, which I associated with being an adult.

Finally dessert was served. Granny liked the sweet and heavy variety, but quite often we had ice cream, made that morning in our kitchen. Delicious! I was then ready for my nap. Sis and I chimed, "May we be excused, please?" "You may get down," Granny always said.

Returning to my home, Hyde Park, that first summer after moving to Seattle, Granny considered my manners needed a good deal of sprucing up. Lunch with her was educational. It wasn't only manners but rather a cultural background she conveyed. "Our background," as she might say. I was taught how to serve myself from a platter held by the butler (and to always say thank you), how to use my knife and fork with some style, when to use the butter knife—and when not to—how to drink from my water and milk glasses. And not to spill anything. But no sense lingers of her instructions or admonitions having been a burden. Even when she corrected my pronunciation or pointedly frowned when I used a questionable expression learned from my public school classmates, I was not put off. I wanted to belong. I wanted to belong with Granny.[3]

I know my mother felt lovingly about her grandmother—in spite of what she would write to her mother, Grandmère, to gain approval—and spoke nostalgically about life at the Big House. Neither of us liked the habit displayed by so many writers of comparing Eleanor with her mother-in-law, Sara, yet that writing of it went a long way toward making such comparisons standard practice.

And I, too, am doing it. To put it simply—considering only one aspect of two complicated personalities—Sara gave of herself freely. Eleanor was always measured, with her internal fear of not doing "the right thing" permeating her relationships with her children. These concerns of Eleanor's surfaced with the appearance of her first child, my mother, Anna. Both Sara and the baby's nurse tried to show Eleanor how an infant should be cared for, easily and without anxiety. But the fears prevailed. "Eleanor was a reluctant and anxious pupil."[4] How to look after babies seemed obvious to both the nanny and Granny. Eleanor's lack of confidence, her unwillingness to try developing a physical rapport with her newborn, must have seemed puzzling to both women. But Eleanor was content to leave it to the nurse. She was afraid even to bathe her own child, explaining that she "didn't know how." In contrast Sara had bathed baby Franklin regularly. She hadn't needed instruction.

3

Franklin Delano Roosevelt and Eleanor Roosevelt

Perhaps the two most important people in my life, certainly the most influential, were my grandparents. As a child I intuited both the closeness and the distance between them after thirty years of marriage, and their relationship so much influenced by my grandfather being president of the United States and my grandmother not just being first lady but an important national figure in her own right. Eleanor Roosevelt was known across America as "Mrs. Roosevelt" just as much as Franklin Roosevelt was FDR. How they arrived at this juncture in their life together is an intriguing story.

When Franklin and Eleanor Roosevelt became engaged, there was not much to mark it as unusual. Within New York's upper class, she was, as Theodore Roosevelt's niece, somewhat better known than he. Perhaps their only distinction—outside of their shared social background—was that they both were Roosevelts, she from the better-known Oyster Bay branch of the family and he from the much smaller Hudson River, Hyde Park family. They were fifth cousins, once removed. While they had met briefly as children, they had seen little of each other until Eleanor's debut in society when she was eighteen. She was tall, nearly six feet, with an elegant figure. He too was tall, just over six feet, and handsome.

Their letters to each other showed the usual longing of engaged couples to be together. They couldn't wait to be married. Each saw the other through the rosy lenses that accompany infatuation. When married in 1905, in New York City, their union was blessed by no less than the president of the United States, the bride's uncle. "Let's keep the name in the family," Theodore Roosevelt quipped to Franklin as he gave the bride away.

Both Eleanor and FDR were serious, thoughtful people, full of idealism. They harbored high expectations of each other when they were betrothed. And this can be said to be true of many couples looking forward to a life together of happiness and compatibility. The young Roosevelts' expectations of each other were much shaped by their upbringing.

Relaxed intimacy of any kind did not come easily for those with Eleanor and FDR's Victorian background. Nor was it supposed to. Within their social circle chaperones were always required to accompany a young lady, and to be without one raised suspicions. As a result young couples had very little opportunity to be alone. If a pair was thought to be "serious," it produced worried expressions. Eleanor describes these constraints in her autobiography: "You never allowed a man to give you a present except flowers or candy or possibly a book. To receive a piece of jewelry from a man to whom you were engaged was a sign of being a fast woman, and the idea that you could permit a man to kiss you before you were engaged to him never even crossed my mind."

A certain romantic intimacy demonstrated by a couple was smiled at and viewed with indulgence, but it was not considered to be a good basis for a successful marriage. Social background—coming from "a good family"—and financial stability were seen as far more important in that regard.[1]

It was more than just social norms, however, that restrained Franklin and Eleanor as newlyweds. They both had had exceptional childhood experiences that left them with an idealized and simplistic view of love and marriage.

But if marriage was referred to in romantic terms, any sex associated with this romance was for the purpose of procreation, for having babies and raising a family. Otherwise the subject was not mentioned. Letter writing, however, was a notable exception wherein longing, even erotic passion, could be expressed.

The bride was normally kept in ignorance until the marriage bed. A mother wouldn't have known what advice to give to her daughter except "Do your duty, dear"—which is exactly what my grandmother said to my mother. For a woman to find sex pleasurable was morally questionable, and certainly not a suitable response for a lady properly reared.

When it came to my grandmother, one could feel her reserve with any physical contact. Even when I was a child and my grandmother was middle aged, I knew I should avoid spontaneously reaching out to her. Later I noted her reticence about participating in competitive sports, even tennis, learning that only recently had she felt confident enough to go swimming and ride horseback.

My grandmother had endured a strict upbringing, a typical late nineteenth-century background that was full of "dos and don'ts"—so guilt-inducing!—but these also helped instill in her the lifelong values she exhibited. She remembered little or no intimacy in her childhood except with her father, an intimacy he encouraged that was romantic, totally unrealistic and really quite neurotic. Still, she clung to it feeling that it was all she had.

As a child Eleanor was rarely invited to join her parents in their life. Her mother, Anna Hall Roosevelt, presented an aloof attitude that intimidated her, and I suspect she knew to be very careful when her desire for contact led her to want to touch her mother.

Eleanor and her younger brother were orphaned when she was only nine, and they went to live with their mother's parents. Even then, she reported no sense of affection with either grandparent. Her grandfather had engaged a clergyman to live in their house; hence there was a lot of reading from Scripture. Discipline and proper behavior were expected.

Oddly enough, for a person of her background, my grandmother never wrote about nor mentioned being attached to a nanny or a nurse, although this was quite normal for children whose parents often spent very little time with them. Nurses and governesses were purposely placed between children and parents. They were there to provide daily attention, to carry out the routines and the dirty work entailed in childcare, and to keep the children properly occupied. Indeed these women brought up the children more than the parents did. Under those circumstances it was quite common for a close relationship to develop between a nurse or governess and a child. But apparently this was not so for Eleanor.

Ferreting out Eleanor's expectations of her new husband is difficult, but I surmise what seems obvious, which is that she desperately wanted someone to fill the gap left by the somewhat unsatisfying love between herself and her father. Such expectations were obviously unrealistic. Franklin, who was barely twenty-one years old, could not possibly be a father figure for her. FDR himself wanted a companion—in many ways like his mother was for him—a supporting person requiring a maturity that was quite beyond Eleanor's reach.

Most historians write of Eleanor Roosevelt's "difficult childhood," and my grandmother, when recalling her childhood, reinforced this impression. But looked at realistically I can also see that the "neglect" from which she suffered was not uncommon among children from that milieu. Parents handed their offspring over to nurses and governesses with relief. Eleanor was less an exception than she may have thought.

But the "poor Eleanor" image persists. My grandmother constantly implied that she had had a difficult time because her peevish mother held her at arm's length. In contrast, she never revealed anything less than devotion toward her father, Elliott Roosevelt. In conversation, she might allow that she had been aware of "his limitations," but when acknowledging his weaknesses—alcoholism and drugs—her remarks were always made with sad but affectionate indulgence.

Her closeness to her headmistress at Allenswood School in England, when she was sixteen, provided probably the nearest thing to maternal affection and approval that Eleanor ever experienced. Marie Souvestre was a freethinker but highly disciplined, demanding that her students apply their minds. Eleanor responded well to this rigorous approach—I feel she welcomed it and enjoyed being challenged. She was recognized at last.

My grandmother delighted in regaling us with stories of vacation periods with her headmistress. It is well recorded that Mlle. Souvestre adored Eleanor, who became her favorite, although this was not an introduction to lesbianism as other authors may imply. For my grandmother it was a new and wonderful experience to have an adult person acknowledge that she had a good mind and also for her to be encouraged to use that mind.

Indeed, Mademoiselle insisted on this. Being given special recognition within that teacher-student relationship was a real bonus. Eleanor was very pleased with her life at Allenswood, and hence was most distraught when her Grandmother Hall ignored her pleas and insisted that she return home after only two years abroad. She was to "come out" in society, an experience Eleanor dreaded.

The supporting relationship Eleanor had had with Mlle. Souvestre was an exceptional one. But, upon returning to America, my grandmother retreated back to the childhood experience of life with its familiar built-in loneliness. She reverted to being unable easily to express personal affection except by demonstrating her caring through action—to do for others—and through these demonstrations she would feel she was being responsive. This was typical of her class, of her social contemporaries, and not just one of my grandmother's own behavior patterns. It was part of the pattern of behavior for many of her generation and class of women.

It was their accepted style, as well as a rationalization for avoiding real intimacy.

Good form was practiced through charity. Many women of Eleanor's background limited themselves to expressing care for their spouse and children by planning and organizing the household, reviewing with the nurse what was on the day's schedule for the children, and by other concerns such as seeing that the children were properly dressed, had a haircut or a new pair of shoes, and it was of great importance that meals were prepared and served properly for their husbands.

I suppose it was safer not to put more than your foot or your toe into the pool of love and affection. And by so doing you remained in control—or assumed you did.

Not even later on in life, when she had children of her own, could my grandmother really give of herself and provide the normal maternal intimacy children always hope for. My mother told me the way she and her brothers had shared their sense of neglect by exchanging "amusing" stories. At the same time, however, she always noted how their mother did truly care for them, was attentive to their physical needs, only by her nature unable to hold them close. I remember hearing my mother and uncles in the White House joking together about their mother's close engagement with people across America, her capacity to so freely give of herself *to others*. They concluded that the farther away a person was, the easier it was for their mother to open up. But behind this humor, I felt their ongoing sense of deprivation.

On entering her marriage, Eleanor had been reticent but proud, indeed quick to take offense at criticism. This led to an avoidance of ever feeling vulnerable, of being afraid where it might lead. For her, vulnerability meant loss of control, and that was the primary concern. No doubt she was in love with Franklin, but her instinctive reserve dominated her personality, and was always a barrier between them.

Her shyness went deep, and as a result, she rarely showed or shared emotion except as an underpinning for an intellectual statement. Indeed she had strong feelings, especially when her principles were at stake, but most often, when young, these were kept within her. Letters to close friends were an outlet wherein Eleanor felt greater freedom to express both her love and her frustrations.

She wrote about her sense of inadequacy in her autobiography: "I had painfully high ideals and a tremendous sense of duty entirely unrelieved by any sense of humor or any appreciation of the weaknesses of human nature. Things were either right or wrong to me, and I had had too little experience to know how fallible human judgments are." Later, when she was more than fifty years old, my grandmother acknowledged to her friend Lorena Hickok, "Something seems to be locked up inside me." Before she died, possibly as an apology, she acknowledged the same to my mother.

In my observation, only during her very last years did my grandmother begin to let down her guard and give of herself, as she did with my younger cousin Nina, sympathetically counseling her on how to best cope with her two alcoholic parents.

Like Eleanor, Franklin was generally shy, not the figure exuding supreme confidence we remember as president of the United States. As a young man he was not "one of the boys," yet he presented himself very differently. Up front he was gregarious, the life of the party, always engaged in making a good impression. He wanted to belong—which he wasn't always successful in doing, as is shown through his rejection by Harvard's prestigious Porcellian Club. (My own guess here is that he was judged to be trying too hard.)

Unlike his wife, Franklin was an only child, and very close to both his parents, particularly to his mother. His father and mother were exceptionally attentive to him. The pictures of James taking a very young Franklin riding when he did the rounds of his estate properties show an example of this. But Sara's caring attentions, while loving, could be a bit too abundant. Indeed, some of FDR's biographers have labeled him a mama's boy.

At about the age of ten Franklin was invited to share in some of the adult aspects of his parents' life. This was unusual intimacy for a time when maintaining strict differences between generations was the norm. He accompanied them sightseeing when traveling abroad, and joined them at cards at the end of the day. James, Sara, and Franklin were often a threesome.

The ebullient FDR quickly made friends wherever he went, but I expect it only went just so far. The James Roosevelt family was a tight little island, quite exclusive, and his unusual closeness to his parents required young Franklin to play a particular role. Being elevated to the position of their companion, and invited to participate in his parents' activities, forced him to be a little adult. Somewhere along the line he must have acquired the habit of watching his step, which inevitably led to his limiting any show of more normal youthful feelings. It is impossible to guess at how much he found it necessary to keep personal emotions and exuberance hidden, or how ingrained that habit became. In Robert Sherwood's biography, *Roosevelt and Hopkins*, Sherwood refers to FDR's mind as "an impenetrable forest," but I judge that a bit over the top. There are broader explanations.

That James and Sara gave so much time to their only child, Franklin, was exceptional, especially when compared to many of their contemporaries. Sara Delano Roosevelt got down on her knees to bathe FDR while his nurse stood by ready with the towel. For a time in which servants routinely did a child's bath, it was a unique situation. Nothing like this, not even remotely as far as we know, ever happened to Eleanor. Being kept at arm's length was her lot. And hence it was the style she adopted with her children.

My great-grandmother, as I have said, was known for doting on her only son. And he basked in the attention; indeed he counted on her faithfulness throughout his life. This single-minded devotion of his mother's was an anchor for FDR. True, he sometimes felt her close attentions as tiresome interference, but it did not spoil the mother and son's dedication to each other. When she died in 1941, my grandfather grieved deeply. Indeed it is the only time noted when he wept. In memory of his mother he wore a black armband for the following year on all his suits.

I believe Franklin hoped—and why not?—that his wife would follow suit in devoting time and attention to him, that she would share his dreams and provide the same uncritical support that his mother had represented, the same kind of unstinting support a political candidate typically requires from his spouse.

At one of the annual book fairs hosted by the Roosevelt Library at Hyde Park, I was asked how long it took Eleanor and Franklin to view each other more realistically, free of those rosy lenses that had accompanied their courtship and engagement. I paused for thought and then replied, "About three weeks, I expect." There was a roar of laughter, but it had not been my intention to amuse the audience, nor to be flippant.

When Eleanor and Franklin entered into marriage, each came armed with complicated expectations, both for themselves and of their partner. Compounding this they had little in the way of experience with intimate relationships, and probably none at all regarding sex. Young men of FDR's position might have tried prostitution (certainly not an intimate exchange), and as for young women, sex was considered a marital obligation in those days, one that excluded any pleasurable sharing of the experience. Not only did they lack experience but they were also laden with misinformation—such as the notion that only prostitutes *enjoyed* sex.

During their courtship, FDR enthusiastically shared his hopes for a bright political future. He presented himself as a "reformer," interested in raising the lot of those "less fortunate than we are." Undoubtedly, Eleanor was enthusiastic in her response. She had had direct contact with the down-and-out in a settlement house and thus had more firsthand observation of poverty then had her husband, though she had no activist plans or ambitions for herself. Those would come later, much later—in her middle age.

Upon returning from a European honeymoon of several months, Eleanor found herself in charge of their new home, a small brownstone between Park and Lexington Avenues, 125 E. Thirty-Seventh Street, in Manhattan. She tried very hard to be a good wife in every respect, but admitted that she was woefully unprepared take on this responsibility.

Franklin had said openly that he expected to have a large family. Each had a modest income that would be shared in order to support the large brood they—or he anyway—envisaged. And they knew they could count on his mother, Sara, to top up their finances when necessary.

At the time of their marriage FDR had not yet even started law school, and had never held a job. This lack of employment was the key reason his mother wanted to delay his marrying Eleanor. Otherwise she was not against it; she liked the idea of the link to Theodore Roosevelt. And FDR probably knew that even with his mother's reservations about his early marriage she would fill in the financial gaps in order for the young couple to live in the style of life to which they were accustomed. Throughout their marriage they always had nurses and governesses in tow. In reality their income, when put together, was quite adequate, but my great-grandmother still had to step in regularly to pay expenses such as school fees and trips abroad.

Even though Eleanor wanted desperately to be found competent in domestic affairs, the fact was that she wasn't very well prepared for the practical side of married life. She was not comfortable acting as hostess or running a household with servants. Raising children was a matter of great anxiety. She wrote openly about not knowing what to do, and was obviously very afraid of not doing things right. Criticism, even when merely implied, did not sit well with her.

She wrote: "I had high standards of what a wife and mother should be and not the faintest notion of what it meant to be either a wife or a mother, and none of my elders enlight-ened me." Myself, I find this most odd, as "training" for one's future responsibilities upon marriage was routine for young women of my grandmother's upper-class background. It was an integral part of being well brought up. She continues: "I marvel now at my husband's patience, for I realize how try-ing I must have been in many ways."

In letters written early in her married life, Eleanor lamented her lack of knowledge about organizing and dealing with household staff, ordering the food, and all the other attri-butes and duties expected of a young wife. This ignorance led her into an unrealistic dependency on her mother-in-law, which Eleanor later bitterly complained about, as if it were Sara's fault![2]

It was the same with the children's nurses. Eleanor writes that she let them decide everything because she "didn't know how to." She declared: "I had never had any interest in dolls or little children and I knew nothing about handling or feed-ing a baby." Sara must have wondered (at least I do) if her daughter-in-law had been born without the maternal instincts that normally guide a woman. My guess is that it was fear of engaging physically, and a fear of failing to get it right, and hence opening herself to criticism.

But in spite of early misgivings about being so depen-dent on her mother-in-law, Eleanor very much hoped that attention from Sara might help fill in the gaps of her own at-arm's-length upbringing, giving her the love and atten-tion she had missed. Her letters to Sara when first married show a craving for attention, and also seeking to cede con-trol. It seems to me that my grandmother was in quest of a mother figure just as much as she needed a reliable pater-nal one. She later wrote: "I was growing dependent on my mother-in-law, requiring her help on almost every subject and I never thought of asking for anything that I thought would not meet with her approval."

I have indicated that as the married Eleanor and Franklin

got to know each other, they were undoubtedly disappointed. I suspect FDR had hoped for a partner more confident and more emotionally mature, not so subject to moodiness, as my grandmother admits that she was. Franklin admired his fiancée's independence of mind, her high-minded values, and her unselfish attention to others, but he was now faced with the fact that his dear Eleanor's emotions were quite unpredictable.

I am sure that my grandmother would have liked to adhere to the upper-class norm of her the time—maintaining cheerfulness in all circumstances, no matter how down in the dumps one might feel. But she did not find practicing that dictum easy. For example, just after she and FDR had moved into their New York house, a gift from Sara, Franklin found Eleanor weeping at her dressing table. Her explanation in reply to his bewildered query was to say that she "didn't like living in a house which was not in any way [hers]." But just read the letters from my grandmother to Sara and Franklin, asking them to make all the decisions relating to the building and furnishing of the new residence. In her autobiography she admits: "I left everything to my mother-in-law and my husband." But today the story about not liking to live "in a house which is not in any way mine" is often repeated to show Eleanor as the injured one. Yet it simply is not accurate.

I have said that Eleanor would fully acknowledge that she woefully lacked confidence, and to compound that malaise, turned to stoical silence if she felt criticism was even implied. "One of my most maddening things, which must infuriate all those who know me, is this habit, when feeling hurt or when I am annoyed, of simply shutting up like a clam, not telling anyone what is the matter, and being much too obviously humble and meek, feeling like a martyr and acting like one."

When her third child, a boy, died at eight months old, my grandmother felt very guilty and went into a slump of self-recrimination. "I made myself and all those around me most unhappy during that winter. I was even a little bitter against my poor husband who occasionally tried to make me see how idiotically I was behaving."

Writing about the early years of marriage, she reports: "But those first years I was serious and a certain kind of orthodox goodness was my ideal and ambition. I fully expected that my young husband would have these same ideas, ideals and ambitions. What a tragedy it was if in any way he offended against these ideals of mine—and, amusingly enough, I do not think I ever told him what I expected." Amusing it wasn't, not for Franklin.

He also found that their companionship had limits. For example, he thought they might play golf together. But he was not tactful and commented after one game that she decided to play no more. She never did. "My old sensitiveness about my ability to play games made me give it up then and there. I never attempted anything but walking with my husband for many years to come," she states in her autobiography.

Early on in their marriage, I expect that FDR had also recognized that his wife was unable to fully offer what he most wanted—affection and approval. Likewise, Eleanor's disappointment in her husband's limitations must have surfaced quite soon. She was instinctively judgmental, while his own appetite for approbation seemed limitless.

Franklin's inability to provide her with little more than good-humored affection has been hinted at in my grandmother's writing. Gregarious he might have been, but his notion of intimacy may have been limited to a hearty laugh, a peck on the cheek, and briefly holding his wife's hand.

As with most married couples, the passion of infatuation is a "sometime" state, perhaps lasting only three weeks, or maybe for three years. Then adjustment is required, and to accomplish it there must remain in the marriage a genuine capacity to share feelings. I do not find that element in my grandparents' relationship as man and wife. Both craved an intimacy—but one suited to his or her needs, of course. Yet, sadly, one might think, they couldn't find it in each other. To a great extent their good manners and having both been well bred carried them through. As far as I observed, my grandparents were always warmly polite, never even slightly rude to each other, and they tried to be mutually considerate.

The stress of married life increased when, five years into their marriage, Franklin was first elected to public office, as a senator in the state legislature in Albany. This was a success that much encouraged his political ambitions, his first leg up. Although she felt nervous about her new role as a politician's wife, Eleanor did not object to setting up house in Albany. As she writes, she plunged into her new obligations with great energy, trying hard to fulfill the expectations of a rising politico, and also to raise her growing family. FDR established his reputation as a reformer—and set himself against the "bosses" of Tammany Hall.

Three years later, in a real step up, my grandfather was appointed by President Wilson to be assistant secretary of the navy. The Roosevelt family, with three children, Anna, James, and baby Elliott, and an entourage of servants, moved to Washington where they would spend the next eight years. For FDR, it was a dream come true. Eleanor, on the other hand, was not all that pleased. It meant a new (and fearful) set of duties for her, those expected of the wife of a senior government official. Protocol in the nation's capital was strict and its officialdom was omnipresent, even though Washington was still in many ways just a sleepy (and segregated) Southern town.

Despite her innate good manners, Eleanor felt severely put to the test. However, she managed to rise to the demands upon her. She had to be very correct, she writes, when dutifully making the rounds of the wives of other government officials and noted that she also had her role as hostess for Franklin and her children to attend to. She found the protocol duties boring, tedious, and tiring, adding that she was frequently fatigued, "either pregnant or just recovering" during that time—with three children already and Franklin Jr. arriving in 1914 and John in 1916. As I mentioned earlier, before Franklin and John there was another child who lived only a few months. Hence my grandmother carried through a total of six pregnancies.

FDR simply loved the navy—he always had. By all reports he not only enjoyed his job, he performed it well. I expect he could feel that he was on his way, a young man of great political promise.

Compared with Albany and its politicians forever absorbed with maneuvering, the government crowd of the nation's capital was far less parochial. In Washington, Eleanor could engage in discussions of current issues with the company her husband invited home, people from the diplomatic corps as well as government officials. She especially enjoyed the diplomats, finding them good company. The Roosevelts themselves were also much in demand.

One might assume that Eleanor would be pleased to be so engaged, but that was not always the case. Perhaps fatigued and overburdened, my grandmother began to show self-pity, a character trait that most biographers ignore. Her "Griselda moods" reappeared (she had given them that name after the character in folklore known for her patience and obedience to duty). In spite of the interesting social life that engaged her, she felt neglected and lonely, and somehow humiliated. Yet I cannot see that her life was much different from the other wives whose husbands were either diplomats or government officials. My grandmother would recoil at the thought of self-pity, but it is far more descriptive than the phrase "Griselda mood," which she would use to describe her darker states of retreat.

A typical humiliation—in Eleanor's mind—occurred one evening when she returned home alone from a gay party, having chosen to leave her husband enjoying himself swirling partners around on the dance floor. On arrival she found that she did not have her house key, so she sat down on the front stoop and waited for FDR to eventually return home. Seeing her, he was appalled and perplexed. She had only needed to ring the bell, as he pointed out, and wake up the household staff to let her in. Eleanor, however, apparently preferred to make a scene.[3]

Adding to her tensions was, I suspect, the fact that Franklin was not all that sensitive to his wife's emotional suffering and apparently failed to perceive her loneliness. There were many people in Washington, including relatives, with whom Eleanor could have developed close friendships, but she didn't. Some people from the diplomatic community were definitely of "her class" and she writes of maintaining correspondence with some of them after leaving Washington. Nonetheless, no real companions emerged to share her life in Washington and to relieve her sense of being apart.

In their exchange of letters, my grandparents usually addressed each other as "Dearest Honey," but the distance between them was apparent if you read between the lines. FDR used his duties, especially as the First World War developed in Europe, to stay over in Washington while Eleanor and the family either went to Hyde Park or to Campobello Island for the summer. He joined up with them periodically but for only brief periods.

However, when he was present, either on vacation or in their home in Washington, FDR was a devoted father. My mother and uncles often recollected the fun they had together, with their father leading them in games and roughhousing. Time spent with him may have been limited, but it was very special. My uncle James, the eldest son, remembers FDR's arrivals at rustic, isolated Campobello Island as the start of "whooping, romping, running, sailing [and] picnicking" with their father. My mother, the eldest child and only girl, told me of the efforts she made to keep up. She may well have become a tomboy in her desire to be part of the gang. Her grandmother, my Granny, called her as much—and it wasn't meant as a compliment!

But despite the often lively relationship with his children, I see Franklin as still innately reserved, holding a lot within himself. As noted earlier, since childhood, he had practiced "watching his step" and I expect it continued so, especially with Eleanor. Outwardly, though, he remained gregarious and engaging, and had many friends.

For FDR the opportunities of a political career were always beckoning. He took time off from his government position in 1916 to compete in the Democratic primary for a Senate vacancy but Tammany Hall beat him. Politics, of course, would never be far off in the atmosphere of the Roosevelt household.

He enjoyed having friends both old and new in Washington and continued to be devoted to his work in the Navy Department. He was very busy, engrossed in his responsibilities, yet after a long day would still have energy to spare. Even if he wanted to relax, he looked for amusement to relieve the grind. He needed company—his nature was exuberant—and turned regularly to the Washington social whirl, where he was always welcome.

During this period, especially during the summer months, Franklin would be alone in Washington for weeks on end. After ten years of marriage he knew that the most he could expect from his "dearest honey" were modest expressions of affection and concern for his physical welfare. They were both lonely, but, I think, simply kept any awareness of this to themselves.

Perhaps following Theodore Roosevelt's style of "the vigorous life," they both seemed to glory in keeping occupied, filling every moment of the day—not a word about boredom was ever exchanged. It would have been "poor form." The opposite of keeping fully occupied was to be considered lazy. God forbid.

Washington was a small place; everyone knew everyone. Who Franklin Roosevelt might escort to a soiree was observed, but it wasn't exceptional for him to bring along one of society's single ladies. Lucy Mercer would have been included as one of these "acceptable" evening partners for Franklin.

When Miss Mercer entered Franklin's life during the summer of 1916, she and her mother were well known to be people of "good breeding" but, unfortunately, with a social standing they could barely afford to keep up. While not falling into the category of "gentile poverty," they had strained resources, and this was common knowledge. Lucy had taken a part-time job as Eleanor Roosevelt's social secretary, and she was often invited to dinner at their home if an extra woman was needed. Among the Roosevelt circle of friends, it did not raise eyebrows if she accompanied Franklin socially when Eleanor was away. The young Roosevelts were known to be a devoted couple.

But with sharp-eyed onlookers such as Eleanor's first cousin, Alice Roosevelt, around, Lucy and Franklin being often seen together would not go unnoticed. Observers like Alice might have noted, "perhaps a little too frequently?" She, in short, would have concluded that something was up. And so it was. Franklin and Lucy had fallen in love, deeply in love. It may have been my grandfather's first experience of being head over heels.

Considering Franklin's natural reserve, and the close eye he kept on his future political career, the situation must have been overwhelming. But I can guess that he was quite aware that such an emotional response to Lucy was fraught with imponderables. Perhaps it was her uncritical acceptance of him that entranced him, just as he had always dreamed a spouse would be. Lucy offered admiration and affection in a natural and unaffected way. Whatever the case, FDR was smitten. Caution was thrown to the wind.

Whether they were physically intimate— and this we will never know—is not that relevant in my view. Personally, I doubt it, for Washington's small upper-crust circle was very visible, and FDR's tall figure in his bowler hat was easy to spot. As a senior official in the Wilson administration, he was well known. Undoubtedly the fondness of Miss Mercer and Mr. Roosevelt for each other was noted, but they must also have been much on guard, trying to maintain a proper front—no matter how difficult this must have been for two people so infatuated.

If Franklin thought about it, as I suspect he did, he knew that he did not want to be divorced from Eleanor. But in such situations, clear thinking about consequences is usually not what happens. That FDR could meet a person with whom he could share intimate feelings must have bowled him over, offering him a totally new experience, and one he desperately wanted to hang onto. Still, I'm guessing, he knew it could not possibly be sustained.

As might be expected, the affair eventually came to the surface. The jig was up when Eleanor found love letters from Lucy to Franklin when unpacking his suitcase upon his return from an official trip to Europe. FDR had been seriously ill, and on arrival in New York he had had to be carried off the ship on a stretcher. Delirious from his illness he must have forgotten about the incriminating correspondence in his suitcase.

Soon, news of the revealed relationship made for high drama in slumberous Washington. And Cousin Alice Roosevelt led the pack in this gossip-starved little society. No doubt my grandmother felt deeply hurt, feelings that remained buried within her even after FDR had promised to end the affair and never see Lucy Mercer again. In later life, talking with her friend and biographer Joseph Lash, my grandmother would dwell on FDR's disloyalty.[4] She was, she told Lash, "deeply hurt, and remained so." In other words, she never really forgave Franklin. Yet what Eleanor described as "hurt" was more accurately, I feel, a deep exposure to humiliation. One she never forgot.

The sad fact, however, is that while politeness and good form were always maintained in their marriage, the more than ten years of unresolved tension between Franklin and Eleanor had made the time ripe for Mercer—or another woman—to make an appearance in his life. I offer the above simply as an explanation of FDR's behavior, not as an excuse. There is no ignoring that her husband's affair with Miss Mercer caused my grandmother great pain. Franklin's mother, Sara, was horrified and fully supported her daughter-in-law, saying that she would cut off all further financial support for her son if he divorced Eleanor—which was something that Eleanor had offered. (A perfunctory gesture, I feel sure.)

Historians cite FDR's political ambitions and the continual need for his mother to top up the family's finances as the basic reasons why Franklin decided to maintain his marriage. Both are accurate, but they form only part of the picture. While the overriding reality is that FDR had no future as a divorced man, either financially or in politics, I think, too, that, deep down, he cared a great deal about his large family.

These realities, however, mask a more subtle point. Franklin's rash reaching out to another person for affection and approval might be understood, even condoned, by today's standards. However, in that era, divorce was a social disgrace, surely leading to very awkward situations, with friends disapproving and taking sides. Being in love is one thing, finding a way to live with this love is another. Such circumstances may be routine today, but it certainly wasn't the case in 1918.

Both Franklin and Eleanor were very conservative when it came to social form, particularly with institutions such as marriage. I don't think separation or divorce could ever have been carried through by either of them. They were both raised to endure and to make the best of things. And so they did. Their marriage was to continue but under constraint, and in a different mode.

My grandfather's affair with Lucy Mercer continues to leave me puzzled. He always had a shrewd sense of his political position—his political future—and he was quite open about his ambitions. I cannot imagine that the practically minded Franklin Roosevelt did not occasionally pause in his infatuation and wonder about this. The only explanation is that infatuation is indeed blinding.

On the other hand, my grandmother's writing and her repeated comments to Joe Lash, indicate to me that her resentment, and the continual replay of her feeling so, was devoid of any sense of her own role in her husband's loneliness. She saw herself as the injured one. Franklin had broken their marriage vows—as simple as that. For Eleanor the violation of the vows was a betrayal. All too true. But recognition of her own limited capacity to give of herself in the marriage never seems to have crossed my grandmother's mind. (And I never heard of anyone suggesting it to her.)

FDR was not alone in his frustrations with his wife and his feelings of loneliness. My mother and uncles also felt keenly about their mother's limited approach to mothering. She brought this element of her personality, her innate reserve, into her marriage, and neither children nor husband, nor life experience over the years as a wife and mother altered it. In conversation with a noted psychiatrist later in life, Eleanor commented that she saw Franklin as "the comforter" and her role as "the disciplinarian" in the family.[5]

Writing later, she acknowledged that she hadn't been a very good parent, yet she gave no explanation other than her inexperience—the "not knowing how," as I've said, and feeling nervous about picking up her baby for fear she would drop it. (My grandmother ruefully acknowledged this to me one day as we were discussing my having gone to a "father's class" at New York Hospital when anticipating my own daughter's arrival in the world.)

Eleanor's plight wasn't helped by Franklin always being circumspect in his thoughts. If not an "impenetrable forest"—Robert Sherwood's description earlier cited—everyone agrees that he was not an open person. Indeed, no one writing about him can ignore his limited capacity to reveal the inner man—in sharp contrast to his up-front charisma, the overt charm that marks the memory of him for most Americans.

When in the aftermath of the affair he had settled into a "normal" relationship with Eleanor—although a different normal—Franklin continued his political career, hardly missing a beat. In 1920 he was chosen to run for the vice presidency alongside the Democrat presidential candidate, the Ohio governor James Cox. Campaigning was exhilarating for Franklin. Touring the country and making friends all over America, he quickly became a national figure. Eleanor joined the campaign train once for a brief period, but she kept her distance from the glad-handing of politics. She preferred to stay with the children, she said. Unfortunately, the team of Cox and Roosevelt was doomed to failure; their support of the League of Nations was not popular, and after the First World War and eight years of Woodrow Wilson in the White House, it was the Republicans' turn to occupy the Executive Mansion. The Democrats' defeat was fully expected. But the campaign had made for a large step forward when it came to the political career of Franklin D. Roosevelt. He was now recognized as a political figure on the national scene, with a future that seemed assured.

After the election, FDR returned home to New York City and entered the world of business to provide the necessary income for his family. It was trying. After eight stimulating years in Washington in the thick of government politics, the return to civilian life and working for an insurance company, as he now did, must have been boring. He was making good money, but in no way did it compensate for the excitement of a senior post in the nation's capital. Continuing the tedium, he engaged in the expected "noblesse oblige" endeavors during his free time, the activities that help keep out-of-office politicians in the public eye. Among many other things, he headed the fundraising for the Cathedral Church of St. John the Divine and chaired a supervisory committee for the Boy Scouts in the New York area. All routine.

However, in New York the revised marriage relationship of Franklin and Eleanor led to my grandmother expressing a new independence. In spite of still rearing at home several small boys—aged four, six, and nine, with one more in boarding school—as well as my then teenage mother, Eleanor, upon returning to New York, stepped free from being confined to raising children and the usual hostess duties entertaining Franklin's circle that had been her obligatory routine in Washington.

She now made friends of her own. Her first close acquaintances were Esther Lape and Elizabeth Read, both intellectuals who carried on professional careers but who made it a point to fill their lives with books and discussions about the political issues of the day. (Theirs was reputed, I was told, to be a "Boston Marriage," a companionship of two women committed to each other, as if married.) My grandmother sat at their feet, enjoying the new freedom, and finding a place for herself. It was quite a different scene from the usual cocktail hour–dinner table conversations dominated by FDR. Read and Lape encouraged Eleanor to accept a role that saw her reporting on the state legislature in Albany for the League of Women Voters. She did so and very successfully. As Eleanor writes, she began to find within herself a new confidence.

All this change had barely emerged in the Roosevelts' lives when another crisis hit. Franklin was stricken with poliomyelitis during the summer of 1921. It was serious from, the start, initially crippling the lower half of his body, then it moved upward, stopping just short of his heart, and finally leaving him unable to walk, paralyzed from the hips downward. Normally it was children who were polio's victims, but here was a politically ambitious man in the prime of his life. FDR would never walk again. He had enjoyed trout fishing, had been an active golfer, a tennis player, and an avid dancer; all that now became impossible. Even playing strenuously with the children, occasions that both he and they so loved, would be limited to sprawling on the living-room floor, wrestling.

In the immediate aftermath of his contracting polio, when he was very ill, moving any part of his body was painful. Eleanor's response to her invalid husband was to assume the role of nurse, one that was stressful and soon was exhausting her strength.

For the next eight years, FDR concentrated on efforts to recover feeling in his lower limbs—devoting all his energy to trying to achieve any movement that would indicate progress. But despite the intensity of his dedication to his goal, his physical therapy garnered nothing. When swimming in warm pool water he would experience the sensation of movement in his legs but, alas, it was illusory, caused mainly by the buoyancy of the water. He put on a good front, especially if anyone was watching him perform his painful exercises. Within himself, however, he was depressed—and understandably so for a man whose only ambition in life, a political career, had just been shattered.

Except perhaps for the regular visits of Louis Howe, there was no one really to talk with about how discouraged he felt. As Geoffrey Ward quotes FDR's secretary, Missy Le Hand, "There were days on the *Larocco* [FDR's rented houseboat in Florida] when it was noon before he could pull himself out of depression."[6] At the same time, it is clear to me that choosing to live on a houseboat in the sunny South was also a means of distancing himself from the rancor between his mother and his wife. My grandfather liked to be surrounded by cheerfulness and amusement, or at least a pleasant atmosphere. He disliked unpleasantness. No matter how much Franklin loved his home, life at Hyde Park was no longer congenial.

Luckily, the insurance company where he worked kept him on the payroll even after the polio attack, although the job, what he could do of it, remained of little interest. Only politics ignited him. FDR had always put forward his unabashed ambition to be president of the United States, and meant it. Being struck out of the only game in life that matters to you cannot help but be devastating, agonizingly so. What was left to him was his stamp collection, any charitable work, and his correspondence with former political peers. Governor Al Smith appointed him chairman of the Taconic State Park Commission, something thought a suitable recognition for this ex-politician who, Smith felt, now wouldn't even be able to run for dogcatcher.

Out of a sense of duty, I suspect, my grandmother would make a perfunctory visit whenever her husband repaired to his boat in Florida. She was ill at ease, slept on the deck due to the crowded conditions, and kept her visits to the *Larocco* brief. Her life remained very much focused on New York, where both the children and her friends engaged her.

At Louis Howe's suggestion, Eleanor began to do some politicking on FDR's behalf—as a way of keeping him alive in the public's eye. To help prop up her husband's spirits, she joined Howe in supporting the notion, the hope, of his returning to the political arena. Yet she felt it was a fantasy, given the extent of his disability. Rather, it was about keeping his attention occupied, and was certainly better for him than merely vegetating at Hyde Park with nothing except his hobbies and tree planting. In fact only Franklin Roosevelt and Louis Howe were convinced that FDR would make a return to active politics.

After his brief turn as a vice presidential candidate, FDR had been considered a rising star in the Democratic Party. But now, losing the use of his legs meant he had become a man on crutches, dragging himself along. His former cronies visited, always polite and encouraging, yet they all considered him a political has-been. In their estimation he was finished. The condescension FDR endured from people like Governor Smith must have been galling.

Franklin's illness naturally had resounding implications for his family. My mother told me of the difficult time she and her brothers had. They felt left out. The two youngest were only five and seven years old when they watched their father being carried in a canvas sling from the shore of Campobello Island onto a small boat to be ferried to the mainland. From then on, their time with him would be curtailed and measured by their father's limited energy. Gone were the days when he would lead them through the woods on paper chases. FDR tried whenever possible to include his children during this period of rehabilitation. He talked openly to them about the effects of polio upon his body. He invited them to join him on vacation on the houseboat in Florida, and subsequently at his cottage in Warm Springs, Georgia. But for the children it was nothing like their previous romps with him. They could see that their father's concentration was focused on his recovery efforts.

With her husband's support, my grandmother concluded that the best way of helping him was to assist him with his efforts to stay alive on the political scene. It was also a way of forming a new and useful relationship with her husband while continuing to see her friends and expanding her budding confidence. She was attending meetings and making speeches on FDR's behalf. What followed was recognition—and in her own right—of Eleanor as a competent and politically savvy person. If not quite a political pro, she was demonstrably not just useful but good at helping to organize the Democratic Party for an election.

She quickly became chairperson of the Women's Division of the New York State Democratic Party, and the editor of their publications. There she had met and become fast friends with the head of the women's division, Nancy Cook—and her partner, Marion Dickerman. In addition to her continuing friendship with Read and Lape, my grandmother began to spend a lot of time with this other couple in their home.

My grandfather, concentrating on his physical therapy, was often away for weeks on end. Although my grandmother spoke of trying to be both mother and father to the children, I have often wondered just how much time and attention was given to them during this period. I do know from my mother that it was a period of great anxiety for her and her younger siblings. Polio was mysterious, and considered by many people to be contagious. (Its victims might be relegated to living in isolation in the attic.) When I had a brief illness in 1948, probably influenza, it was diagnosed as polio, and I was actually hospitalized for a few weeks because it was still considered to be contagious by the Los Angeles public health authorities.

My grandmother was increasingly in the company of Marion and Nancy, who seemed very pleased to have the companionship of Eleanor Roosevelt. (While Nancy and Marion were obviously, so I was told, a lesbian couple, Eleanor attached herself like a third wheel—but not of the same diameter.) Nancy and Marion would join my grandmother at Hyde Park when FDR was there having a rest between his therapy sessions. He said he enjoyed their company because they could talk politics.[7]

I remember well "Aunt Marion" and "Aunt Nancy" joining us at the Big House in the mid-1930s for a meal, even though it was a time long after my grandmother had distanced herself from the close friendship she had previously had with them. Early on in her friendship with Cook and Dickerman, in the mid-1920s, Eleanor had mentioned her wish for a place in the country that all three women could share. So Franklin suggested building a cottage for them, near a stream called Val-Kill, on land owned partly by him and partly by his mother. A small Dutch colonial stone house was built that today is open to the public as part of the historic sites at Hyde Park. Franklin himself made the original sketch of the plans and followed closely the construction. (If you visit, ask the Park Service guide to show you pictures of the cottage before John Roosevelt made several additions—a big dormer and the enclosure of the porch.) My grandfather's attitude toward my grandmother's newfound friends I find most unusual. He welcomed them—as simple as that—never expressing any reserve toward them.

Whenever her husband returned to the Big House, Eleanor dutifully joined him, keeping the small room next to his as her bedroom. Otherwise she would be working in New

York City or on the weekends at Val-Kill cottage with Nan and Marion. She was, as always, busy, busy, busy.

Granny's response to her daughter-in-law's new friends was more reserved but not unfriendly. After Val-Kill was occupied by Marion and Nan—and as a weekend place by Eleanor—Sara sometimes noted in her letters that Eleanor was often not at home where, Granny felt, she belonged. But there was never any overt friction, and my great-grandmother was always a gracious hostess to Nan and Marion, as both women would confirm.

That Eleanor did not feel "at home" in the Big House is well known. But what is often forgotten is that Sara was the matron—the owner—of Springwood, and would continue to be so until she died late in 1941. When staying there, as I often did, it was obvious that Sara Delano Roosevelt was the mistress of the Hyde Park estate. She ran the household. She regularly made the rounds of the property, just as "Mr. James" had done, until she was in her early eighties.

No, it wasn't Eleanor's home. Yet living with one's mother-in-law could be quite normal—as it could be to have adjacent houses, as the Roosevelts did on Sixty-Fifth Street in Manhattan. Even that was not that unusual. (My grandparents had been married in the double house of cousin Henry Parrish.)

With regard to Eleanor's new relationships—with Esther and Elizabeth as with Nancy and Marion—I see my grandmother stepping out on her own, expressing her independence by establishing close, indeed loving, relationships with these women. As such it couldn't help but be a very significant period in the development of Franklin and Eleanor's marriage. FDR was giving all his energy to trying to recover some use of his legs, and he still hoped to return—someday—to active politics. But he needed his wife, and she was responsive in very practical ways. In this crisis they learned to be supportive of each other. I see the period from 1920 to 1928 as the time for feeling out and developing the partnership that would be further developed when Franklin returned to public life, eventually occupying the White House.

Throughout this period my grandmother continued to have her own life, her own friends, and her own work. She wrote extensively for popular magazines, and by the time Franklin returned to politics as governor of New York in 1928, Eleanor was, in fact, making more money than he was. But she always carried out her "wifely" institutional responsibilities at the governor's mansion in Albany just as she would do in the White House in Washington—all the while maintaining at full speed her own activities.

As governor of what was then the biggest state in the United States, Franklin's return to active political life found him a much tougher man—as well as a more sensitive one. His eight years of therapy for his polio may not have produced any improvement in his physical condition but it had taught him patience, fortitude, and humility. In practical terms he would learn a great deal more during those four years as governor, 1928–32, for the Great Depression had just settled into America. FDR tested his political strength, his views widened, his confidence increased.

As a politically aware spouse, Eleanor now offered valuable support. She was already well known within the New York State Democratic Party, and now deemed a professional by those who had worked with her. Many years later when I accompanied my grandmother to Paris for the 1948 session of the UN General Assembly, I watched the other members of the U.S. delegation and its staff being terribly surprised at what an experienced politician Mrs. Roosevelt seemed to be. They were completely unaware of her honed political experience gained even before FDR became president.

In spite of their stresses and difficulties, or perhaps because of them, Eleanor and Franklin's marriage did evolve into the partnership that so many people have written about. As far as I know, this mutuality wasn't anything they ever talked about; both just implicitly understood it. Quite unlike other prominent political couples, particularly recently, the Roosevelts relied on their shared values and practiced restraint in order to understand each other. It was more than a profound respect for each other, far more than a front of politeness. Each trusted the integrity of the other. Eleanor and Franklin shared a common heritage, beginning with their Victorian background, and this continued as a guide for their marriage and behavior. At times it weighed heavily on the latter part of the vow, "for better or for worse." But I emphasize the "for better" as the relationship evolved.

Indeed the partnership blossomed further, taking on a new dimension during the White House years, 1933–45. In my view my grandmother found that being "Mrs. Roosevelt" was an identity that fitted her perfectly. She now had a reputation of her own across America, and of course her influence as the wife of the president. The partnership of Eleanor and Franklin was tacitly recognized by everyone in Washington. They were not a "team," but they worked together in a complementary way.

An extraordinary example was Eleanor being trusted with the task of going to the Democratic National Convention in 1940 to speak to the rancorous delegates who were about to deny FDR's choice for the vice-presidential nomination. Key Democratic Party leaders had been urging FDR to come to Chicago, but he wouldn't budge from Washington. So they pressed Eleanor to come. Naturally, she asked her husband if he wanted her to go. In her autobiography she wrote of his reply: "It would be nice for you to go, but I do not think it in the least necessary." Eleanor then repeats to him what party leaders had been saying to her and asks, "If Jim Farley asks me to go, do you think it would be wise?"[8] FDR replied, "Yes, I think it would be." (These are my grandmother's recollections. Why was my grandfather being so coy, I wonder? Or is it my grandmother pumping up another good story?)

Eleanor Roosevelt's address at the convention was brief,

quite extemporaneous. (She recalls having jotted down a few phrases on the back of an envelope.) It was made up of generalities but with many implications—and the delegates got the point. They agreed to nominate Franklin's choice of Henry Wallace. Soon afterward, FDR telephoned to say that he had listened to her speech. As she modestly reported, he told her "that [she] had done a very good job." I remember the smile on my grandmother's face as she told this story.

One question, regularly asked, remains—especially by those who would attribute much of the New Deal to Eleanor Roosevelt's efforts. How much influence did she have on her husband, the president? This is one of those "iffy" queries to which no one has a definitive answer. Primarily from talking with my mother and grandmother, I conclude that Eleanor's influence with her husband varied from one issue to the next. On some, her opinion carried great weight, while on others very little. Not a brilliant analysis perhaps, but it does make sense if you appreciate FDR's sense of timing in politics, which was a major element of his thinking process, one he always kept to himself.

Throughout, one basic variable was always in play: If it was a political issue on which my grandfather and grandmother agreed, and one for which FDR could see a politically viable way forward, there was no problem. But if it was a politically touchy piece of legislation before the Congress, FDR could be evasive, if not downright secretive. As I say, timing in politics was his game, one he alone knew best how to gauge. I feel it was instinct that guided him. His evasiveness with my grandmother could irritate her no end, so she would shrug her shoulders and then let off steam with my mother or one of her friends.

After her husband's death, my grandmother expressed some amusement at her own frustration. She came to see that her influence was always subject to his game, his canny ways—all of which made him an extraordinary president. Indeed, I suspect my grandfather often did not know what he would do until it felt right within his guts or circumstances forced his hand. And that could be at the last moment!

Another very important element in Eleanor and Franklin's relationship stemmed from the role she played by bringing information and firsthand observations to her husband, usually from sources that would not otherwise have been available to him. Often there were simply poignant letters she had personally received from individual Americans, or significant conversations she had had with people hoping to obtain her influence with FDR. Also it was her extensive traveling across America that enabled Eleanor to see firsthand how our country was faring. Because of her travels she was able to offer her husband a wide perspective. And, most importantly, he trusted her views. She always said that it was he who had taught her to be such a perceptive witness.

Eleanor saw her husband tête-à-tête at his bedside every morning, usually just before his staff arrived for the morning briefing, and also in the evening, before he relaxed with his mystery story. By the time she became first lady, Eleanor had had a long experience of gathering information for her husband. She knew he valued her observations and her assessment of situations. People like Robert Sherwood put it forward that one always "got through" to the president via Mrs. Roosevelt, but, as my grandmother would be the first to acknowledge, this wasn't always the case. She writes in her autobiography: "I know Franklin always gave thought to what people said, but I have never known anyone less influenced by others." Always modest, she chose to ignore the substantial influence she had with FDR.

With her sharp eye and wary judgments ("You have to taste the food dear," she would advise me, "not just ask what the menu was."), I see my grandmother as indispensable for FDR. Since he had become a cripple and was unable to get about to see things for himself, she had turned herself into a very good reporter for her husband. She detested the press labeling her as the president's "eyes and ears," but it wasn't far from the truth. FDR talked with many people but it was to his wife's perceptions, to her continuing accounts of the world beyond his own, to which he attached considerable credence.

Thanks to Eleanor's keeping her ear to the ground, her husband was better informed than most presidents. People don't realize that all presidents are very quickly blocked in by their White House staff, who wish to act as gatekeepers, using their own regular access to the president to, as they imagine it, protect him. Especially from information they weren't controlling. FDR countered this by giving direct access to his many contacts across America, men and women he'd come to know, dating back to his 1920 vice-presidential campaign, often to newspapermen whose views he valued, with his wife being principal among his sources.

Additionally he used her popularity with the public—as well as with those who loathed her—to test new ideas or approaches on thorny social issues. The quality and quantity of the comments or flak she often received, particularly from a hostile press, proved a useful gauge for FDR, guiding him as to how far he could advance this or that policy.

Whether her intervention concerned citizens out of work or those blocked by the bureaucracy from obtaining a benefit to help them survive the Depression, or took on such broad issues as racial hatred—epitomized by the lynchings in the segregated South—the press, or columnists like Westbrook Pegler, would chastise the first lady for not knowing her place. In response, she invited Pegler to lunch at Val-Kill for her frequent Sunday barbecue. There were enemies who called her a "nigger lover," particularly after she invited Marian Anderson to sing on the steps of the Lincoln Memorial. This was when the Daughters of the American Revolution had forbidden her to give a concert in their Constitution Hall.

In the early years of their marriage Eleanor and Franklin were what I would term conservative. Neither were much involved with the revolution in social patterns that began to evolve in the early days of the twentieth century, ones often sponsored by the Roosevelts' upper-class peers like Dorothy Whitney. While definitely interested in social issues, they did not join social-reform groups—Eleanor avoided being a suffragette for example. At the same time, they had always been "liberals." According to my dictionary's definition of the word, it is, roughly, a generous attitude toward other people. To be liberal was both a view of life and the way one felt about the people who shared your life. That's certainly the understanding I have of my heritage.

By World War I, Franklin and Eleanor had begun identifying their liberalism with specific political and social issues. For example, they supported President Wilson's progressive views and his efforts to gain Senate approval of America joining the League of Nations. But one can best see FDR's growing political liberalism during his term as governor of New York State from 1928 through 1932. The Great Depression, then coming into full swing in American life, focused his sense of the important role government needed to play in aiding its citizens mired in economic distress. In contrast, President Hoover had been flatly against government intervention in the economy, despite the onset of the Depression. Only in his last year in the White House did he begin to change his view.

Figures like Frances Perkins and Rex Tugwell widened FDR's awareness, just as Molly Dewson and Harry Hopkins broadened Eleanor's. Across the board she was now active in supporting liberal issues. But both Roosevelts were never doctrinaire; they avoided ideology or rigid thinking. This was especially true of FDR, who wanted to let his mind roam to explore a variety of options—from whatever source.

Nevertheless, in my view, my grandparents never moved far from their fundamental cultural orientation—the upper-class form and parameters that had shaped their outlook since they were young. He enjoyed equally the White House and the Big House of our Hyde Park estate. The title of a book, one written to damn FDR, *Country Squire in the White House,* was not far off the mark.

And yet it would not be inaccurate to refer to him, as his detractors did, as a "traitor to his class." Why? He was both the leader of the New Deal and a country squire. Sharing the president's background, the first lady could also have been labeled a traitor to hers. My grandmother's background and early training also always marked her, even when she was visiting miners several hundred feet down a shaft. Perhaps today's politicians should note: most Americans didn't seem to mind my grandparents' obvious good manners. Both were simply true to the best of their origins.

Her husband's health had long been a major issue in their marriage, from the day he contracted polio until the day he died. FDR's continuing effort to regain feeling in the lower part of his body was always on his mind. ("Even in one toe!" he quipped to my mother.) But he achieved nothing, no improvement from all the therapy he underwent. Her husband's condition preoccupied my grandmother continually—even when they were apart. She was on the telephone daily to remind him to do his exercises. Yet it was his health that had pushed Eleanor out into the political arena, where she learned to enjoy "the game" and its challenges.

My grandfather continued to hope that a magic bullet might be produced, a way to reverse his paralysis. Even as late as the end of 1944, only a few months before he died, Cousin "Daisy" Suckley arranged for an Indian "healer" to work on Franklin's legs. My mother, Anna, was invited to be present at the therapy session—indicating to me her father's own reservations—which was carried out in his bedroom in the White House. Nothing came of it, just as with all of his previous efforts.

A year after his coming down with polio—when he was in physical therapy and concentrating exclusively on regaining some feeling in his legs—one of his therapists suggested that my grandmother stop telephoning daily to nag her husband about doing his exercises.

In 1932, when FDR had just been elected president, my grandmother faced, or refused to face, going to Washington as first lady. She was dismayed. Despite her significant role in the achievement, she didn't like having to give up her own work in New York, teaching and politicking. From her previous exposure to the White House—both during Uncle Ted's administration and in Woodrow Wilson's—she saw no reason to look forward to presiding over never-ending White House receptions, affairs at which she would have to be polite and smiling. This life, she knew, would bore her stiff. In New York she had interesting work and lots of friends. With these friends, she was quite open in bemoaning her soon-to-be-taken-up role as first lady. Louis Howe, FDR's *éminence grise*, ordered that one of her letters to Nancy Cook be burned, owing to its bluntness about her despair over the imminent move into the White House.

But I don't feel this brief drama—quite overplayed by historians in my view—posed any real question about her continuing partnership with Franklin. She was disappointed when he declined making her his secretary. I wonder if she'd been really serious in suggesting it. So in what had become her usual way, she looked to her own resources. The result would be the legendary "Mrs. Roosevelt." In short order Eleanor Roosevelt had found for herself a very satisfying role, an identification that fully suited her.

The partnership between Franklin and Eleanor, as I've indicated, was not always smooth sailing—far from it. At times, my grandmother was a bit of a "hair shirt" for her husband. To put this in a more positive light, she forced him to think about matters he might have preferred to avoid.

For example, during the election of 1944, Eleanor relentlessly pressed FDR to get out and actively campaign against his opponent, Governor Dewey. Franklin refused to budge from the White House because, he said, his role as commander in chief, his responsibility for running the war, was his priority. And that's where the American people expected him to be. Not until the last four weeks before the election did he campaign—and he then won very handily. Thus proving his point, I would say.

Toward the end of the war, when my grandfather was already in poor health, my grandmother was not always sensitive to his growing fatigue. She might harangue him over supper about a domestic issue she felt was of critical importance, but one he didn't feel had the same priority for him as overseeing the immense war effort. My mother once intervened, saying, "Mother, can't you see you're making Pa ill?" Indeed, Franklin finally had to limit the number of items Eleanor could put into the basket on his bedside table, materials she wanted him to go over before he went to sleep, not even allowing him the possible respite of some lighter reading.

As some readers may know, Lucy Mercer did reappear on the scene—and without my grandmother's knowledge. Perhaps Franklin felt his promise not to see her again had been limited to the near future after they had parted. In the late 1920s he and Lucy had begun to correspond occasionally. In 1933 he invited her to view his first inauguration as president from a White House limousine parked near the Capitol where he would take the oath of office. He did not actually see her, however, until early in the 1940s when he visited her on her estate in New Jersey—Lucy was by then the widow of Winthrop Rutherfurd, a wealthy stockbroker. It is not generally known that throughout this New Jersey visit, which lasted several hours, Margaret "Daisy" Suckley, his distant cousin, accompanied FDR.

Later, toward the end of World War II, my grandfather more than once invited Lucy to visit him at the White House. They went on drives through Rock Creek Park together and had lunch or supper, meals at which my mother, Anna, was usually present.

In fact it was my mother who was burdened with the duty of making the arrangements with the Secret Service and the White House staff for Mrs. Rutherfurd's visits. She felt great guilt about this, torn between not wanting to do anything behind her mother's back and yet following her father's wishes. We had returned to living in the White House by then, and my mother was functioning as FDR's personal assistant—unpaid. Her office was in her bedroom, with a card table serving as her desk. But a great many telephone lines!

She told me later that she recognized her father's increasing loneliness and his great need for convivial company during this period of extreme personal stress. His role as commander in chief during the war was exhausting—twelve hours a day, seven days a week. Understanding this, she felt that the most important thing she could do to help keep him going was occasionally to provide company he could relax with.

Indeed it had been my mother—not my grandmother—who had insisted, with Admiral Ross McIntire, the official White House physician, a nose and throat specialist, that a cardiologist be brought in daily to monitor her father's heart condition. Dr. Howard Bruenn had been instrumental in making the diagnosis of FDR's heart problems several months earlier and he now became his attending physician.

When FDR died at Warm Springs on April 12, 1945, Daisy Suckley and cousin Laura Delano, along with Lucy Rutherfurd and Elizabeth Shoumatoff, who was there painting FDR's portrait, were all present. Mrs. Rutherford and Mme. Shoumatoff left quickly enough. My grandmother arrived from Washington as fast as she could. Cousin Laura sidled up to her and reported sotto voce that Lucy had been present. My grandmother nodded and moved on, not wanting to give our gossipy cousin any satisfaction. But she did confront her daughter upon returning to the White House. My mother's explanation did not assuage Eleanor's pain—and her feeling of being humiliated again. But although the rift between mother and daughter was quickly healed, the hurt remained inside both of them; for many years it was something neither woman talked about except for my mother's explanations to me, which I have noted above.

As my mother and others had often observed, Franklin Roosevelt enjoyed his role in the White House from the day he arrived. He liked being president. He liked being the focus of attention. It fulfilled his dreams—and considering that he had been decisively written off as a potential candidate when crippled by polio, it was an unheard-of achievement. Would we elect a cripple as president today? And do so four times in a row?

My grandmother would come to find the White House useful, although I never heard her directly admit it. She remained detached, always saying she would be glad when she could leave there and return home. Yet there's no denying that her position as first lady provided a platform that launched her as one of the most influential women of the twentieth century. More importantly, her reputation for courage and integrity was such that these personal hallmarks followed her all through her life. Four presidents and one vice president (Lyndon Johnson) attended her funeral in the Rose Garden at Springwood in 1962, where she was buried next to my grandfather.

"Mrs. Roosevelt" was still her identification in 1948 when I was with my grandmother in Paris for the United Nations' General Assembly. When I remarked on her extraordinary popularity with the French people, her reply was, "It's all because of Pa, dear!" I don't feel that she meant to be humble, or in any way demeaning of her own achievements. It was only simple recognition of the fact that if my grandfather hadn't been president, she would not have been first lady—and thus able to benefit from the opportunities available through occupying the White House. I think she fully appreciated this element of the relationship they had shared.

Whatever your view or opinion of their bond—"the partnership of Eleanor and Franklin Roosevelt"—it has become a legend. I regard these two people, both separately and together, as having provided us with unprecedented political leadership. They influenced how the American people developed, how we endured the Great Depression, and how this country carried on through World War II. When *Time* magazine chose a dozen people as "the most outstanding" of the twentieth century, *both* Franklin and Eleanor were among them.

Some historians reduce Eleanor and Franklin's relationship to functionality, simply a utilitarian use of each other for political purposes, yet I personally observed the quiet affection and deep respect they continued to have for each other. Of course, their partnership was useful to both, but it grew out of, and was maintained by, their commitment as a married couple.

Their bond in the later part of their marriage did not suddenly blossom in the White House. Rather it had emerged after much travail. As a married couple theirs was a long road, a slow process of emphasizing the positive in an exceedingly difficult marriage—and it could easily have taken a different turn, one not conducive to developing a partnership. But a common heritage and the values they shared shaped the course of their long union. Over the years, they instinctively found ways of supporting each other. Only too well did they know the flaws of the other, but the many things they had in common moved them to continue working together, and caring for each other.

How do you describe a relationship, a marriage of forty years, especially when for nearly fifteen years their home was that bustling overheated palace of rumors known as the White House? The husband was the most active and perhaps the most skillful president of the century. The wife was also bent upon continuing her own interests, but found—and without calculation—that being First Lady was an extraordinary stage from which to do even more effectively what she truly desired to do. Eleanor gave of her time and imposed upon herself a strenuous schedule. Her style and prodigious energy set a precedent for all future first ladies.

The White House provided the opportunities but also the

limitations, the unique box within which my grandparents had to make the most of their partnership. FDR did what came naturally to him. As president he was our leader. In her own way Eleanor was also our leader. Review the profound influence she had upon many Americans, especially American women, and continued to have even after her husband died.

It was an extraordinary marriage. Without hyperbole, it can be said that the American people gained greatly from their relationship. The leadership they provided, both separately and together, was dependent upon their relationship as a couple. That the marriage endured is one thing, but that it prospered in its own particular way—and under the glare of public life—is quite unusual. It had its obvious limitations and periods of rockiness but these did not stand in the way of doing what was necessary to "get on with it." They adapted and adjusted. They remained committed to each other as husband and wife, and as partners. Is not this steady devotion a form of love?

4

White House Pleasures of the Table

One of the comforting things about life in the White House was the regularity of some events—like teatime in the afternoon, at about 4:30. Sis and I would be dressed up, looking proper with hair combed and all in place. But while I much enjoyed the tea and cakes, it was being included in the adults' company—and also being the object of a good deal of attention—that appealed to me the most.

In the evening the president presided at the dining table. My grandmother, as his hostess, sat opposite him. Even in the so-called family dining room, the table was quite large and easily seated twenty people, so the distance across the table between them was at least ten feet. Yet no matter how crowded the table was, Franklin Roosevelt's personality prevailed. But at teatime my grandmother was in charge, my grandfather rarely present.

When I was young many American families still followed the English tradition of afternoon tea. Granny daily had tea at Hyde Park, even if she was alone. There was always tea at the White House. It might be for a few of us gathered in the West Sitting Hall or a reception for several hundred on the first floor of the White House.

If it were only a dozen of us, Eleanor would be there behind her lovely old tea service ready to ask, "How would you like your tea?" My grandmother was very proud of that service, for it had belonged to her own grandmother. (Once, in an expansive mood, she gave it to her second son, Elliott. He promptly sold it and she had to buy it back from the gallery whose owner, Victor Hammer, was, luckily, an old friend.)

At teatime Eleanor would request the company of those she wanted to see and talk to. The West Hall on the second floor, the family quarters, was screened off from the elevator and hallway and made an informal enclave. By that hour the butlers would be in tails with stiff boiled shirts and white ties. Around a table in the middle of the room, chairs were set casually about. Little tea tables would be placed near each.

Her guests ranged from old friends to newspaper reporters she liked, and also family, like my sister and me and our mother. There might well be several newcomers. Some guests might be scared stiff, wondering how to behave when having tea with the first lady in the White House. But whether friend or stranger, it was an invitation you did not turn down.

For my sister and me it was always an occasion not to be missed. We looked forward eagerly to the pleasures of such treats as the delicious pound cake and my own favorite, cinnamon toast. But what equally mattered, as I've said, was the opportunity for us just to be there. Otherwise, I never sat at table with our family—not until I was nine and Sis was twelve years old.

At teatime I encountered people from all over the country and, occasionally, foreign visitors as well. The atmosphere was subdued but intense and the conversation, often about serious issues, was always good-humored. Any laughter was polite, restrained, and suitable for the occasion. Everyone was on their best behavior, acting as they thought they should. When family members were present, they would sit back and allow Grandmère to lead the conversation—and care for her guests. "Tea with lemon or milk? And sugar?"

Eleanor Roosevelt also made use of these occasions to entertain people that she might not wish to invite to dinner.

(Supper with FDR made for a different sort of social occasion.) The teatime guests, though, might be selected for many reasons: for example, they might be persons to whom she felt an obligation, or those who had had experiences she wanted to explore. It was at tea that I met Mr. and Mrs. Walter Reuther, Mary McLeod Bethune, Frances Perkins, and Harry Hopkins. There would also be complete strangers, whom my grandmother had run into and found interesting on her many journeys to the four corners of America, and to whom she had said simply, "If you're ever in Washington . . ."

While not lacking in discrimination in her invitations, it was nevertheless clear that she paid no attention to class or educational background. My grandmother simply responded spontaneously to those to whom she felt drawn, anyone who intrigued her in some way, whose story caught her imagination.

There might be ten or more people turning up, or just as possibly only a few. It could wind up an odd mix. There was one afternoon, a year after we had moved into the White House, where those assembled were only Sistie, age seven, Buzzie, age four, and the Polish ambassador, just the three of us with my grandmother. As Grandmère later reported to her friend Joseph Lash, she "read poetry to the assembled."

Among the selections I remember—certainly eclectic—were Noyes's "The Highwayman," Keats's "Ode on a Grecian Urn," Milton's sonnet, "On His Blindness," and Kipling's "Danny Deever." All were over my head. I wonder what the Polish ambassador thought.

When Sis and I made our entrance into the West Hall at teatime, escorted of course by our nurse, everyone stopped talking. Introductions were made all around. Our nurse, as custom dictated, would withdraw. Sis and I, well trained, said "How do you do?" to each guest, and then sat down, our places indicated by a nod from our grandmother. She then poured weak cambric tea for the two of us, with not too much in the cup as it had to be carefully balanced on a very small and delicate high-legged table next to the chair. We sipped slowly as we'd been taught to do, and I tried not to eat too greedily the cake that had been passed to me by the butler. Fascinated with the details of my own contained world—as any little boy is—I noted that these small tea tables, off of which we ate our cake, came in sets of three or four, one fitting under the other, like a nest. That seemed very clever to me.

Only once did I disgrace myself—at least, that was the way it was viewed—by spilling in my lap the small cup of very hot tea I'd been given. Actually it was quite a painful burn, although not a serious one. It was a few weeks before I was again allowed to join my grandmother for tea.

Looking back, it seems amazing to me that we would be expected to eat a full supper so soon following tea and pastries. But, after it was signaled to the nurse that our appearance as Eleanor's guests was over, up to the third floor we went. From the basement kitchen came our meal, brought up by the creaking pantry elevator. The cart carrying it was rolled in by another of our "buddies" from the staff. I liked the "repartee" we shared—silly, but just right for setting me off into giggles.

We ate what was put before us, never complaining. Supper, like lunch, was inevitably meat or fish, overcooked, just as were the vegetables—usually canned peas and carrots along with either rice or potatoes. And such a heap of food likely was preceded by a soup! A dessert followed, one of these "sweets" I particularly disliked, and my sister knew it. She would gleefully describe the tapioca we were served as "fish eyes and glue," and then enjoy my look of distress.

Just as often a dish of sickly sweet, tinned fruit, cut up into small pieces, was presented. Quite awful. Bread pudding was marginally better, though it seemed to me little more than stale bread mixed with custard and then moistened with evaporated milk. Occasionally there would be a real treat, ice cream, which pleased me no end. During our supper on the third floor, our mother or grandmother might pop in to chat with us for a couple of minutes before they went off quickly to change their clothes for the cocktail hour. After this brief visit they could report that the children were getting along just fine though neither seemed to be very hungry.

My bedtime followed soon after, quite early by today's standards, probably between 6:30 and 7:00 p.m. Saying good-night, too, was another family ritual. When I'd been tucked in, Beebee would "send word." This message was passed to FDR's study on the second floor where the cocktail hour was still underway. My grandmother, working in her own study, was also informed. She picked up my mother and Missy LeHand from his study, and they all proceeded upstairs.

Gathered around my bed, each intoned the wish that I should sleep well, each kissed me, and then returned downstairs. But once, my response in front of this little delegation embarrassed them all: I'd noticed that Missy had a little dark fuzz on her upper lip, and when she bent over to kiss me good night, I took it into my head to announce, "Missy has a moustache!" Nobody knew quite what to say. There was confusion all round, including my own: it is my first memory of putting my foot in my mouth.

For a child my life was formidable, scheduled to the quarter inch, a formal routine carried to extremes. Still, it didn't bother me. There was a security in knowing what I was doing, or scheduled to be doing, at every moment. It was actually quite comforting.

At age nine I began to eat with the adults. Again, I ate what was served and never thought of complaining. I knew nothing in contrast. My grandmother felt that one should not pay undue attention to food, an attitude picked up by my mother and echoed by my sister. What I liked or didn't like didn't occur to me. When moving out into the world, however, I awoke. And when doing the research for this book, I read how others, including my uncles and mother (secretly), felt that the White House food was really inexcusable.

"Just awful!" commented Harold Ickes, the secretary of

the interior. "We always have something to eat before going to dinner at the White House." In short, the meals at 1600 Pennsylvania Avenue were notoriously poor. The family complained. The president complained. But we had no influence. My grandmother remained oblivious. The first lady would brook no criticism of her housekeeper.

It was a topic always reviewed—and always with sarcasm—when family members got together. My grandfather frequently complained of the unappetizing lunches he was served at his desk. Yet all to no avail. My grandmother blamed it on the squeeze of the small budget she was allowed, but every one of us knew only too well that she was a puritan at heart and didn't approve of such "indulgences" as tasty food. Grand-mère was supported in this by Mrs. Nesbitt who was just as rigid in her own belief in frugality.

We were fully aware that part of the blame for the dull boarding-school style menus lay with the White House housekeeper, Mrs. Henrietta Nesbitt. This woman, whose regime we viewed—as did all the servants—as tyrannical had been brought by Eleanor from the governor's mansion in Albany to Washington, along with her husband, Henry, who became the White House chief steward. Her qualifications for the job were meager, a course in nutrition and food management, its teachings embodied in the phrase "what is good for you." Daily she went over everything with my grandmother. She never did any of the cooking but was responsible for suggesting the menus, ordering the food, overseeing the cooks and organizing the household staff. Considering the many visitors and the frequent receptions, along with three meals a day plus tea every afternoon, her job was not easy. Yet there was no reason for Mrs. Nesbitt's being so strict.

I do wonder why we were always served vegetables and fruit from tins when Washington had open markets. My guess is that Mrs. Nesbitt felt "safe" with the canned goods. In those days everyone assumed that major corporations like General Foods could be counted on for the very best quality. But the canned stuff was awful. The sticky sweet peaches or pears, for example, were my sister's and my standard desert. If by chance ice cream appeared, it was obviously someone's birthday!

Before the war one always heard English food criticized as being overcooked. Alas, ours in the White House was the same. My grandfather liked his meat rare, as did my mother and uncles, but he never saw a slice of lamb or beef on his plate that wasn't very well-done. Covered in a cream sauce, the chicken was tasteless. So were the vegetables.

Although she was aware that her housekeeper wasn't popular, Eleanor simply left her alone to get on with it, adding, or perhaps rationalizing to herself, that Mrs. Nesbitt needed a job. I was told that FDR, when teased about his reasons for wanting to win a fourth term as president, replied that he wished to be elected again if only to have the opportunity of firing Mrs. Nesbitt! In fact, what actually happened was that my grandfather, with my mother's encouragement, finally brought our cook Mary from Hyde Park down to the White House.

A few years ago the Roosevelt Library at Hyde Park opened a cafeteria in the new Wallace Center reception area, and named it Mrs. Nesbitt's Café. So much for history!

5

FDR's Cocktail Hour, the High Point of the Day

From my earliest memories I was aware that my grandfather enjoyed a special event each evening that was extremely important to him. And I was also aware that my grandmother didn't quite approve of the goings-on at her husband's "cocktail hour." Yet the cocktail tradition had been a household fixture for years. I have in my possession my grandfather's "bar," which he used in our house on Sixty-Fifth Street in New York City during the years of Prohibition in the 1920s. It looks like a bookcase when closed. But when opened—there are all the bottles and glasses!

Whether Franklin Roosevelt was at the White House or at his home in Hyde Park, without fail he observed a daily cocktail hour. He dubbed it "the children's hour." But I was not allowed to attend until I had reached the magic age of nine. It was then that I was first included at the dining table for supper, and hence also at the cocktail party that preceded it. From 6:15 to 7:00 in the evening became the highlight of my day; I was included in a select company.

When I was younger I had passed by my grandfather's second-floor study during the hallowed hour, and heard animated voices and laughter from behind the large mahogany door of his study. In my childhood there were many things in which I was not included because I was not yet old enough. I wore short trousers and my jacket had no collar until I was twelve years old. And the only reason I was included at table, and hence at the cocktail hour, when only nine was because my twelve-year-old sister became eligible. And my mother did not want to leave me having supper alone on the third floor. Besides, both family and friends remarked how well-informed I seemed for my age and could converse about current events. This decision annoyed my sister greatly, but she put on a good face to accommodate her three years younger brother.

At the end of a long work day, after leaving the Oval Office in the West Wing, FDR might have a quick swim in the White House pool and receive a brief massage of his useless legs before being wheeled back to the second floor of the White House, the family quarters. He always changed his suit for the evening, putting on a clean shirt and a different tie. Then he was wheeled into the handsome oval study that was conveniently located right next door to his bedroom.

FDR would preside over the gathering from behind his desk, seated in his big swivel chair. Papers had been pushed aside to make room for the large tray of drinks in front of him. Guests assembled quickly, comprising perhaps a dozen interesting people, plus a few family members and friends, mostly people who fit the sort of company FDR liked. Sis and I would arrive with our mother and, after giving our grandfather a hug and a peck on the cheek, move quickly to the sidelines. Because I knew most of the guests, I felt quite at ease in this adult company, and said a polite "Good evening" to everyone in response to their "Hello, Buzzie."

There was an atmosphere of conviviality. Conversation was spontaneous, even noisy, a mixture of lighthearted banter and serious dialogue, but it always touched on politics. I was on my best behavior, listening and taking it all in. Like many well-bred children of my generation, I had been brought up to be "seen and not heard." I couldn't get enough of the exuberant style of my grandfather and his guests and their amusing talk—most of it gossip about what had gone on that day in Congress or in one of the many government bureaus. The day's newspaper headlines and the latest opinions of prominent columnists were also good fodder for conversation. There would be bursts of laughter as the humorous sides of people and events were brought to light. FDR's sallies dominated. These were usually broad observations but could occasionally be quite pointed, even personal, yet all in good fun. That was the style of FDR's cocktail hour. Yes, it was gossipy, but I never heard a really mean word—well, maybe one or two about this or that hostile Republican senator or archconservative congressman.

A cocktail-hour regular, and one well-suited for this atmosphere, was Harry Hopkins. Of course, with his chronic stomach problems he shouldn't have been drinking at all. Nonetheless, he made sure that he got his full quota of martinis. His slanted but engaging smile made it seem as if he was always on the edge of laughter or about to make a sardonic comment. How he could quip! He was one of the most amusing of the crowd. Slouched, leaning forward, a slightly cynical expression on his face and a cigarette dangling from the corner of his mouth—he shouldn't have been smoking, either—his observations always hit the mark, and the funny bone.

When Harry remarried after his wife died, it was to a chic lady named Louise Macy, known as "Louie"—a former correspondent and former Paris editor of *Harper's Bazaar*. He was obviously enchanted with his new wife. He straightened up and tried to look more like the sophisticate he really was. My grandfather too enjoyed Louie's repartee, and she became one of the select few women to whom FDR had a particular attachment. Eleanor tolerated some of these women but not others. Mrs. Hopkins unfortunately landed in the latter category.

She fell afoul with my grandmother when she rearranged the table setting one evening, a task my grandmother always did herself. "Louie" had overstepped, and the first lady so informed her. This was always a danger for women in FDR's social circle. Harry Hopkins himself, I was told, advised the handsome Trude Pratt, soon to be Mrs. Lash, not to get too close to "the Boss" or she might lose Mrs. Roosevelt's friendship. Trude became more circumspect.

More sober—in every respect—was FDR's chief speechwriter, Judge Samuel Rosenman. He could get off a good remark from time to time, though his delivery often was. Perhaps his wife, Dorothy, hanging on his arm, was a dampening influence. Less reserved was Robert Sherwood, a new addition to the select group of speechwriters. But he was more than just a talker; he took it all in—and later published the well-known biography *Roosevelt and Hopkins*.

FDR's military aide and general factotum "Pa" Watson—Major General Edwin Watson—was deceptive. On the surface he seemed a bit of a buffoon, laughing heartily at everyone's jokes, especially his boss's. His face was always wreathed in amusement, but underneath a shrewd intelligence was at work gathering the rumors and gossip being shared, all of which he would assess with FDR the next day. My grandfather rated Watson so highly that he later would make him his appointments secretary. Being a family man, he usually went home after cocktails, preferring to have supper with his wife and children.

Bill Hassett, FDR's appointments secretary at that time, was a quiet man. During the cocktail hour he listened more than he commented, in the same way as his colleague Watson. Despite his reserved nature, he was delightful company for those who came to know him. Of course, he would comment on the evening's conversations the next day if asked to do so by "the Boss."

It was my grandfather's secretary, Missy LeHand, who coined the title "the Boss" for her employer. Having worked for FDR since his campaign for the vice presidency in 1920, and having lived with us as part of the household after my grandfather contracted polio, she had a special place at the cocktail hour. If my grandmother was absent—which she frequently was—and my mother wasn't present, Missy acted as FDR's hostess. Every one of the other guests knew she had probably more influence with "the Boss" than anyone else in his entourage. When it came to repartee, she was quick. (She was like a second grandmother to me. I was a teenager before I knew she had any name other than Missy.) Because of her closeness to FDR, it was all the more remarkable that she was successful in getting along with my grandmother, whose friendship she made great effort to maintain. Eleanor and Missy had a remarkable mutual sympathy and understanding.

My grandmother's response to the cocktail hour was cordial but plainly reserved. She usually didn't make an appearance until toward the end—she had "too many other things to do," she said, and then she would reappear to announce that dinner would soon be served.

No one who knew Eleanor Roosevelt expected her to engage in sophisticated chatter, let alone appreciate the boisterous conversational atmosphere that her husband enjoyed. Somehow, perhaps as a matter of choice, she had not developed a talent for making the amusing remark at the right time. Maybe she felt that such a level of talk tended to diminish the importance of serious matters, and, what is more, that the fun was often had at the expense of other people. True enough: most of the pointed remarks were aimed at someone present, one generally quite capable of shooting back.

During the proceedings, my grandfather would sit back in his big chair—telling stories, making quips, or maybe just smiling, raising his eyebrows, and laughing loudly at the remarks of others. After the first round of his martinis—which were, I was informed, truly awful—he would promptly mix another round, adding four parts gin to one part dry vermouth and then an additional splash of gin—just to make sure he hadn't miscounted. He might also add a few drops of absinthe—"for taste." Swishing it around in the martini shaker "till it was very cold," he would fill up any glass or goblet placed in front of him. Today you can see displayed in the museum at the Roosevelt Library the shaker and some of the glassware and silver goblets used at those cocktail gatherings.

At some point FDR's valet would appear with a bowl of food for Fala's supper. My grandfather's little Scotty would next run over to his master who would take the bowl and hold it in the air, demanding that Fala roll over and sit. Then, and only then, did the president's pet receive his meal. Afterward, Fala, always the performer, would circulate among the guests to be greeted warmly, cadging what small tidbits he could charm from his admirers.

Since I was always the youngest dinner guest, I was, by protocol, the last to leave to descend to the family dining room. As the other guests were bowing each other out, I would discreetly empty the dregs from a martini glass or two, especially if someone had been foolish enough to leave a nicely marinated green olive at the bottom of the glass. Then I would quickly follow my family and their guests, glancing at the seating chart as I went by the second-floor usher's desk to find out whom I would be seated next to at supper. Would he or she be interesting? Or one of the less desirable, which is to say less lively guests whom my grandmother had felt obliged to invite?

Many times during the year, especially in the summer, my grandfather would return along the Hudson River by train to Hyde Park. His daily ritual of the cocktail hour played out quite differently in the Big House. His study there was tiny—it had been the children's schoolroom when my mother and her younger brothers were growing up. About fifteen feet square, it had built-in bookcases that made the space still more cramped. In this small room afternoon cocktails were served.

This was in sharp contrast to Washington, where in the president's White House study, cocktail hour attendees could mill about and mix freely. They had space to wave their arms and gesticulate, using expansive body language to emphasize the point of a juicy story.

In the Big House at Hyde Park there was no room for that. FDR's desk and armchair took up so much space, and there were so many guests, that people were forced to hold their drinks close to their chests—while remembering not to wave their arms! Getting the host's attention for a refill from the ever-ready martini pitcher was a major maneuver accompanied by cries of "Excuse me!" even though it was only a few feet away.

Of course there were fewer people present at Hyde Park than at the White House. Still, the same sense of fun prevailed. My grandfather brought only three or four of his staff from Washington, but family and friends made up the difference. Into this little room we would be packed like sardines, early evening revelers eager for gossip and the infamous martinis. Some didn't stay for supper—our dining table held only twelve people easily—but no one wanted to miss the conviviality of FDR's cocktail hour.

A regular at Hyde Park was cousin "Polly," Laura Delano, from Rhinebeck. She had hair of brushed blue or purple henna with a widow's peak, and she wore so many rings and bracelets that one wondered how she could raise her drink aloft. In contrast was Cousin Daisy: Margaret Suckley, demure but handsome, and FDR's favorite lady. There was also our portly Cousin Leila, who took up twice as much space as Bill Hassett, the skinny appointments secretary, and whatever other family members might be on hand. Too, there could be several Morgenthaus visiting from their family estate close by at Fishkill. My grandmother occasionally brought two or three guests from her Val-Kill cottage, but she herself usually stood in the doorway, both in and out of the game. My grandfather seemed just as happy among this packed throng as he was presiding over the grander cocktail hour in his spacious White House study.

Unfortunately, the delightful "hour" was in truth little

more than half or perhaps three-quarters of an hour. My grandmother set the schedule. Her appearance at the gathering signaled that supper would soon be announced. "Top up and drink up" was what her arrival signified.

Whether at Hyde Park or at the White House, upon the first lady's entrance into Papa's study, the decorum improved, voices softened, and the level of noise noticeably dropped. My mother used the term "a wet blanket" in describing her mother's effect on the crowd. Her brother, my uncle Elliott, simply quipped, "Here comes Mother!"

We were familiar, as were most of the guests, with her characteristic reaction to a slurred voice or a loud guffaw from someone enjoying FDR's martinis a bit too much. This did not elicit even a mild glare of disapproval. Instead her face registered concern for the culprit, coupled with a touch of sadness. Everyone held Eleanor Roosevelt in such high esteem that this expression was sobering enough for all present.

Eleanor Roosevelt's attitude toward drinking and its loosening of the tongue was often the occasion for family amusement. But it was serious; it had a long history, its roots in an unfortunate family affliction of alcohol abuse, one that had affected her throughout her life. It had begun with her father when she was a youngster, and then, as when she was living with her grandmother and two wild alcoholic uncles, and still later with her younger brother. My grandmother thus was intimately acquainted with the behavioral problems created by addiction to alcohol. And she worried about her sons. My reading is that my grandmother had a deep-seated fear that liquor would lead to "loss of control," and this fear, deep within her, was always an important factor in her way of being, of relating to the world around her.

At Hyde Park my sister and I well knew we had to arrive as early as possible for the cocktail hour, lest we get squeezed out of our grandfather's small study. (There was no room for my dog, Ensign, so he stayed upstairs.) With ginger ale in hand, I would position myself on the far side of the room, squeezed up against a bookcase, playing the wallflower, so that when guests dispersed I could enjoy my usual game of emptying the martini glasses and downing the olives.

Both at the Big House and at the White House, FDR's cocktail hour was markedly different from other Washington functions. Usually when its government or business people gather to share a drink at the end of the day, a certain amount of useful information is typically exchanged. This is expected. Perhaps a deal is casually struck, or a congressional leader is able to test the political waters for an amendment to a piece of legislation. At the very least, somebody usually takes being in the company of his superiors as an opportunity to show off, scoring points or just plain swanking.

President Roosevelt would have none of this. For his guests to be working, in any of the subtle or not-so-subtle ways mentioned above, would have been frowned upon. His cocktail time was for relaxation and amusement, and he did his best to gather together people who shared his penchant for fun. It was a ritual, one I will always remember.

6

Eleanor Roosevelt's Book on Etiquette

Even when very young I had absorbed my grandmother's sense of things that were "right" and things that were "wrong," and especially things that we were "against." Being a snob was number one on this last list. Even strong likes and dislikes were questionable. Labeling someone a snob meant that they thought too highly of themselves, manifested airs, or had stilted manners that seemed contrived. Hence Eleanor Roosevelt's choosing to write a book on etiquette was certainly a surprise. But a little background first.

When living in the White House I was told many times—indeed, strongly admonished—"We are not snobs." Implicit was the accepted attitude: *"They* (snobs) are people we do not approve of!" The implication was that we were above that sort of attitude toward other people. Children, as we know, pick up the truth, particularly when their parents are being hypocritical. What was this baloney all about?

I accepted my grandmother's view on snobbery. She strongly disapproved of people who thought themselves better or "above" other people, usually because of their social position, their class in society, or, more likely, their wealth. This was usually expressed, as I say above, through what they considered to be superior manners, haughty airs or a condescending manner, or disdain of the behavior of people who might be considered less "well-bred." They would look down on persons who had not been to "the right schools" or who had a different accent. All that, I was informed, was snobbery. I took it in instinctively, siding, as a result, with the underdog, meaning anyone I observed being sneered at for no good reason.

Even at a young age I could sense the truth behind all this. My grandmother thought it better to pursue a real education rather than learning the correct way to hold your teacup in a so-called finishing school. One can't disagree! When her sons married young women from "the society set," my grandmother tried hard to be accepting, and was always kind to her daughters-in-law. But I remember many a raised eyebrow from her when a snobbish expression came burbling out from one of these wives at family gatherings.

Eleanor Roosevelt actually took against some people she thought were snobs. My mother, always looking for approval from her own mother, followed suit. And my sister was quick to pick this up—with me as her major target. The most deeply felt condemnation (or taunt from my sibling) as I was growing up was the accusation of being a snob. I was an easy target.

As I have mentioned earlier, I was compelled to leave the White House and move to Seattle in 1937, accompanying my mother, sister, and new stepfather, John Boettiger. He wanted to live close by the country club, explaining that he could more easily play golf and entertain business friends there. But it was also where people would expect the president's daughter to live, he noted. My mother put her foot down. "We don't want to associate with that snobbish group!" And that was that. We were *not* snobs.

Furthermore, I was not to go to a private school but to a Seattle public school because, as she wrote to my grandmother, it will bring Buzzie into contact with "less privileged children" and he will make more "regular" friends. In the letter she expresses the hope that "rubbing shoulders with many different types of boys will help him acquire more independence and confidence." (For me it was a disaster, but that's another story.)[1]

"Equality" was the byword in Eleanor Roosevelt's mind—and hence in all of ours. Indeed, if there is a cornerstone to Eleanor Roosevelt's worldwide reputation, it is her stance against inequality and discrimination. I knew from listening to my grandmother that it wasn't just an intellectual position on her part. She saw people being hurt; that is what aroused her. She saw inequality, and especially discrimination, as being injurious.

But even as a child I could look around and see that equality was more of an idealistic value rather than what I observed in the real world. I could see, for example, that my grandfather and my uncles were far less concerned about snobbery. It certainly wasn't a word I heard used by any of my teachers nor any of the kids at the public schools in Seattle I attended. However, in this atmosphere it was made abundantly clear to me that *I was different*.

Moving forward many years to Christmas time in 1962, just two months after my grandmother had died, my mother and I were having a rather somber holiday in Los Angeles. Without Grandmère's taking charge at Christmas time, as she always had, the exchange of presents seemed sadly unexciting to us. In the past, she had been the one to arrange the piles of presents for each of her children and grandchildren in the White House and in the Big House at Hyde Park, and then at Val-Kill. When my grandfather was alive, my grandmother was the one who organized Christmas stockings for everyone to open when sitting around FDR's bed in the White House on Christmas morning—a tradition I will always remember.

Nevertheless, two months after she had died, her presence and presents were still very much in evidence. As usual my grandmother had been buying gifts all year and carefully putting them away in the "present closet," noting on each the name of the recipient. Some of the gifts even had her scrawl on the card, for example: "Buzz—Merry Christmas and Love, Grandmère." One that was not even wrapped as a gift was a package from Macmillan, the publishers. My grandmother had probably given them a list of people to whom her new book was to be sent. Here was mine, and I wondered what it was.

There it was, big and heavy. I opened the package . . . and was startled, to say the least. My beloved Grandmère, Eleanor Roosevelt no less, had written a book on etiquette! It wasn't just odd. It did not fit in at all with my—and America's—image of this person who stood up for what was right, often pointing out in a penetrating way where so-called correct manners were used to perpetuate unkindness or class distinctions. She appreciated good manners but saw etiquette as often being used by one person for putting down another—or just for showing off.

After noting that it was inscribed to "Buzz and Jeanette"—my wife at that time—I put it aside. In fact, I found myself appalled, I admit. Not wanting to read it, I kept it in a bookcase reserved for volumes I knew I would never crack—although I have carried these around all these years as part of my permanent baggage.

Rearranging my books recently—my shelves are overflowing with books on the Roosevelts—I again came across *Eleanor Roosevelt's Book of Common Sense Etiquette*. For the first time, I looked at its table of contents and began to dip into it. Then I couldn't put it down. Memories of my grandmother teaching me manners and values flooded back to me, including her admonitions about snobbery. All was intertwined. My formal manners, how to behave, particularly table manners, came from my great-grandmother, Granny, and these have stood me in good stead. But the manners taught me by Grandmère came from being with her, watching her, the formalities she observed and her innate kindness, melding them together. Her style is vivid in my mind, so natural and unaffected, yet very much reflecting the politeness and consideration of her background. I find it difficult to put into words. And sadly, I must say, no actress portraying my grandmother has ever mastered it.

Style was what set Eleanor Roosevelt apart from other people. I was frequently with my grandmother until I was thirty-three—my age when she died—and as far as I could observe, her own style was exactly the sort people wanted her to have. Nobody seemed put off by her very obvious upper-class background, a style that was already becoming outdated. Indeed the public seemed to relish a graciousness that was already old-fashioned.

What was also unique was the unaffected way my grandmother expressed her manners. There was kindness and warmth, along with the ease that her background—her training from childhood—had provided. Those invited to tea at the White House, where Eleanor Roosevelt presided, would be a mixture of friends, some of them well-known people, along with others whom even she did not know well.[2] Some were obviously shy of being included in Mrs. Roosevelt's tea party, plainly ill at ease. Yet she quickly made them feel welcome and part of the party. In our younger years, if my sister and I were present, we often found ourselves, as her grandchildren, being used as objects of attention upon which all could focus. We were known as the "ice breakers."

My grandmother felt that manners should be used to give style to life. Some people referred to it as "grace." More importantly, it meant adhering to "good form," especially when it might ease tensions in stressful situations. She is quoted on the book jacket summing it up quite nicely: "Etiquette, from my point of view, is not just a matter of knowing how a lunch or a dinner should be served, or whatever the 'proper' behavior is in this or that situation. There are many correct ways of behaving in almost any situation, and many proper ways of doing those things for which there are precise rules in formal etiquette books. But the basis of all good human behavior is kindness. If you really act towards people within your home and out of it with kindness, you will never go far wrong." Thus spoke Eleanor Roosevelt.

But why did my grandmother get involved with such a book? I suspect that one motivation was her desire to strike out against snobbery. She knew of the popularity of books offering rules for what was seen as correct etiquette, authors such as Amy Vanderbilt or Emily Post.[3] She saw these authorities being used by people to reinforce the surface behavior that delineated class differences. Showing up the public's appetite for class distinctions, both books were best sellers for many years, making both their authors famous.

The archives at Roosevelt Library at Hyde Park provide the essential clue about how Eleanor Roosevelt became attracted to this project dealing with etiquette in a new and different way. As I suspected, it had been proposed to her. And it was the editor himself who did the writing. However, the nominal author did put her oar in. Robert Ballou, to whom the book is dedicated, sent his draft to Eleanor and she replied: "It seems to me that you have done a simply wonderful job and I feel very hesitant to change anything, but I must add something to the book or it will be all yours, so I am trying hard to mark the places where I can perhaps make some personal contribution."

I can see why my grandmother had been tempted by the idea. Not only was the book an alternative to the snobbery she saw implicit in the popular books on social behavior by Post and Vanderbilt, it also covered ground that Eleanor was keen to see presented, such as a section on how to behave when visiting a foreign country. Overseas tourism, after all, was already booming among Americans.

There is also a chapter on "Showing your Colors," which expresses my grandmother's views about thoughtless expressions of patriotism, especially relevant in the era of the Cold War. "No amount of flag-waving, pledging allegiance, or fervent singing of the national anthem is evidence we are patriotic in the real sense of the word."

Covering her social views, there is another chapter I especially liked entitled "Keeping up with the Joneses." There is even a section in the book pertaining to behavior with handicapped persons. This reminded me of when Helen Keller visited the White House and I was home from my military school, sporting my fancy uniform. My grandmother brought Miss Keller and her companion to meet me. She wanted Miss Keller to feel the trappings of my outfit, especially the brass buttons. I was about to draw back when I remembered that this special guest was both deaf and blind and that the lady with her was the person who had laboriously taught Helen Keller the limited communication she now had. My internal discipline prevailed, and I smiled politely as Miss Keller's hand roamed up and down my chest.

As her publishers noted in the title, "common sense" is the book's keynote. And my grandmother concludes: "If you ever find yourself in a situation in which following a formal rule would be manifestly unkind, forget it and be kind instead." That statement alone sets hers apart from the usual books on etiquette.

7

Security in and out of the White House

When I was born in 1930 my grandfather was governor of the state of New York. My earliest memories are of our family home at Hyde Park. Men in uniform, state troopers, were as routine a sight for me as were the gardeners and servants who worked in the Big House. I liked the troopers' shiny black puttees and Sam Brown belts that supported their side arms. What I didn't realize is that these men were there to protect my sister and me, my Granny, Sara Delano Roosevelt, and, of course, the governor, whenever he visited.

When we moved to the White House three years later, there were even more uniforms to differentiate—army, navy, marine corps—everyday dress, full dress, and so on. I was delighted and soon knew all the distinctions. But these people were not our protectors. Others were. First there were the White House police patrolling the White House grounds and stationed at the entrances. They looked like ordinary policemen to me with their not very exciting uniforms. They were familiar with the regular visitors who came and went out by the front entrance to the Executive Mansion on Pennsylvania Avenue. My younger uncles would come "home" for a few days during school vacations. It was on one of those times that Uncle Johnnie came rolling in at three o'clock in the morning and the guard didn't recognize him. My uncle had to wait while the man checked with the usher on night duty. Johnnie was most put out and took the matter up with my grandmother the following morning—after he'd slept it off.

More drably attired still was the White House Secret Service detail. (I never received a satisfactory answer to my query about why they were "secret"!) They were dressed in civilian clothes and looked much like other people on my grandfather's staff. Yet, whenever my sister and I ventured forth from the White House, one or two of these people accompanied us. Several of them became like friends to my sister and me.

Until my grandfather died in April of 1945, when I was within a week of being fifteen years old, I had rarely ventured out without some kind of surveillance. The fact was that I was better acquainted with my keepers than I was with any person of my own age. The Secret Service men were my chums, my buddies. I was dependent upon them for their companionship—as well as their protection.

There were good reasons for all this security. The first was the threat of kidnapping. Just as we moved into the White House in 1933, there occurred the tragic case of the Lindbergh baby, whose kidnappers ended up killing him. Later, when I moved to Seattle in 1937, two kidnappings had just taken place nearby. In one instance I remember ransom was paid for the boy's release. The threat to my sister and me was real but we were not made aware of how real it was until much later, when we were teenagers.

The second kind of threat could come from hate groups or from disturbed individuals stimulated to violence. Again, I was only dimly aware of the level of threat such views engendered. When I was thrust into a public school in Seattle I was taunted by a few of my classmates with typical anti-Roosevelt slogans, prejudices passed on by their parents. But this never seemed serious, only bad manners.

What I didn't realize is the degree to which my grandfather was, literally, despised by a very small but vociferous number of Americans. Leading the group were major figures from the business and financial worlds. They started what was known as the America First movement. Also, there were demagogues such as Gerald L. K. Smith or Father Coughlin, whose radio program had an audience of millions. They were not muckrakers but "haterakers."

I was told that some people could hardly speak, so worked up were they when hearing the name of Roosevelt. This made me take notice, trying to imagine persons seized by such uncontrollable emotion. Fanatical hatred was a phenomenon I'd never heard of before or even considered. It seems that my grandfather—inexplicably, of course, to me—provoked this reaction among some people. It was a puzzle.

The Secret Service had their hands full running down these "crazies," especially when they hid behind seemingly respectable organizations. Until I worked in the Roosevelt Library archives doing research for my book, I hadn't been aware how serious it was. I learned that toward the end of his second year in office, and running into the first two years of his second term, 1934 and 1935, a quite serious national effort was launched against my grandfather. It was a phenomenon so disturbing as to be considered newsworthy. Major publications such as *Time* and *Newsweek*, as well as the big city papers, gave it major coverage. It was known as "the whispering campaign." Although it never achieved the influence that the Tea Party has today, it was thought to be a political threat to FDR during his reelection in 1936.

The Hate Roosevelt file in the archives of the Roosevelt Library at Hyde Park is a mixture of the hilarious and the sinister. To delve into it is to realize just how active were the various cabals of Americans that lusted after FDR's blood. Coups were hatched—what the Associated Press termed "Cocktail putschs"—but some were real enough to be exposed before a congressional committee by Marine Corps General Smedley Butler, whom a group of conspirators had tried to enlist in a plot to engage the U.S. Marines in overthrowing the government.

When you read some of the accusations thrown at FDR, you wonder why they were ever taken seriously. A few of the more stupidly outlandish stories went as follows:

"Have you heard his mind's completely gone? He's hysterical most of the time and has fits of laughing and crying that he can't control!"

As one reporter looking into this whispering campaign noted, "Most of the stories are far too obscene to be believed."

At the cocktail hour, as I've said, Franklin Roosevelt mixed martinis, relaxed, told stories, and listened to his friends report the day's gossip. One of his favorite openers was to repeat a new Hate Roosevelt story. "Do you know they've had to put bars over the White House's windows to keep me from throwing myself out?" Roars of laughter all around.

But for the Secret Service, it was not a laughing matter. It was its job to assess how serious these threats were, whether by groups or individuals. Any threats to the president or to the first lady were their primary focus. But my sister and I figured in the picture as being especially vulnerable, just as the Obama children have been.

My family's reaction to the Secret Service's protection of the president's family was mixed. My great-grandmother wouldn't allow any agents into the Big House at Hyde Park. After her death, just a few months before the Pearl Harbor disaster plunged us into World War II, the Secret Service detail began occasionally to use the room next to my grandfather's study. A desk and telephone were installed, although it was not exclusively for them. FDR's secretary, Grace Tully, might use it, and so did my mother. For the rest of us it was just the passageway to the only toilet on the first floor of Springwood. And when you were billeted on the third floor, this was convenient.

Eleanor Roosevelt refused any and all Secret Service protection. She was adamant. My mother and uncles speculated about whether the Secret Service secretly and discreetly tailed her. But no one knew—or wanted to know—for sure.

Following their mother's attitude, my uncles disdained protection, but my mother welcomed it when my sister and I left the White House to move to Seattle. Looking back on those years I see my mother and stepfather using the Secret Service man as a convenient chauffeur to ferry my sister and me around, especially when we began going to different schools or frequently to the dentist.

The Hate Roosevelt phenomenon continued long after FDR's death. In the mid-1950s, ten years after he had died, I was having lunch with a friend, a prominent Republican named Victor Ridder, at the National Republican Club in New York City. Halfway through our main course a man came marching up to our table and asked me in a very demanding tone of voice—loud enough so that all surrounding tables could hear—"Are you Buzzie, FDR's grandson?" My host was most astonished, as was I, but I nodded assent. Whereupon this man announced that he would "not eat in the same room as Roosevelt's grandson!" Then, wheeling about, he left. A perplexed Victor apologized. I smiled, shrugged, and we got on with our lunch.

Yet, like many other things within my extraordinary life as the eldest grandson of President and Mrs. Roosevelt, I took this security protection for granted—from age three to fifteen. It was simply an accepted part of my daily life for most of my childhood and youth.

But I was unaware of its stamp upon me—until my grandfather died. Shortly after that I headed to Chicago and then to New York to be with my grandmother for my boarding school's Easter vacation. There was no Secret Service buddy meeting me in Chicago and accompanying me on the train to New York. No one looking after me. I was alone—and it did feel very strange.

8

Religion in Our Family

Much of this chapter is conjecture because the subject was never discussed openly among us. Often, as I could observe, going to church depended simply on who in our hierarchy was planning to attend. But the subject of religion itself was out of bounds for conversation. It was a private matter—which gave rise to all sorts of rationalizations.

When I was a child—early in the 1930s—attendance at church may have been declining but it was still the norm of society in order to belong. It was the proper thing to do. A century earlier, however, when America was expanding its frontiers to the West, and new towns sprang up across the plains to accommodate the pioneers, carrying a letter from one's previous church to verify that you were a churchgoer in good standing was essential when it came to being accepted by your new community.

I always felt that my grandfather was a deeply religious person. And yet his profound sense of God was never ostentatious. In fact I had the impression that my grandfather tried to avoid going to church if he thought he could get away with it. "I don't like people watching me saying my prayers!" said the president of the United States when pressed by the first lady to attend. A good excuse, I think, but my guess is that, really, the church sermons bored him. He did like to sing, however—singing out, as the Methodists do, you might say.

While in the White House or staying at Hyde Park I joined the entourage at church on Sundays. At Hyde Park I knew—indeed I took for granted—that we had "our" pew. It was marked by a silver plaque inscribed "James Roosevelt." I also was proud of my grandfather's being the senior warden at St. James, a lovely church just across from the Vanderbilt estate in the village of Hyde Park.

At St. James we were "low church." Our rector was not "Father" Wilson but "Mr." Wilson. Indeed any vestige of papism was to be avoided. That meant that all religious display was frowned on, for example, fancy vestments or, heaven forbid, incense. All that was what my mother might refer to as "folderol."

My grandmother, as well as my great-grandmother, were more regular churchgoers than Papa. We always accompanied Grandmère to church in Washington. We would be bundled up against the cold if it was winter or dressed in our Sunday best if it was clement weather. Off to church we'd go, Sis and me, with our nurse Beebee, joining the first lady in the large White House limousine. Sometimes, if it was only to St. John's Church on Lafayette Square just across from the White House, we would walk. But occasionally we went to other churches as both grandparents thought the president's wife should show her respect for other denominations. (I don't think I ever went with our grandmother to a fundamentalist church, though I once did this, taken by my nurse—who was later scolded by my mother for her initiative. For my part, I had been impressed by the enthusiasm I saw there, not the usual subdued reverence I was used to.)

Going to church in Washington with my grandfather I found much more fun than accompanying my grandmother. FDR used his big open car, and he liked having Sis and me in the back seat with him. While sirens were prohibited, this being Sunday, we still had the motorcycle outriders to intervene at the intersections we crossed, as well as the bustle of the Secret Service men running alongside. I liked the roar of the engines and the people waving in recognition, not minding at all their "oohing" and "aahing" and pointing to "Sistie and Buzzie." Riding with our grandmother was much more subdued; she didn't like recognition, she said. I feel she also worried that it might "puff me up." She was right, it did. I enjoyed the limelight but knew not to show it too much. My sister exhibited an indifference she felt our mother would approve of.

Normally, as I mentioned earlier, there was no discussion of religion in our household. One's religious feelings and affiliations were considered private. If occasionally I overheard the labels "atheist" or "agnostic," I knew they were references that were frowned upon—although intellectually tolerated. (Yes, I instinctively understood the distinction.)

When I listened to one of FDR's fireside chats—sometimes sitting in the front row of the few chairs facing my grandfather and his battery of microphones—it didn't seem at all odd to hear him occasionally refer to God. In 1944, when my mother sent me a draft of the D-Day prayer with which FDR would address the nation on June 7, it was indeed nothing less than a prayer to the Almighty. And yet when asked by the press to give forth about his personal beliefs, FDR's limited response was, accompanied by the usual grin, "I am an Episcopalian and a Democrat." Seriously, I would never have dreamed of asking my Papa—or my grandmother—about their religious inclinations. I took the formalities of our limited religious practice for granted, and went along with it unquestioningly. Like referring to sex, talking about God or Jesus was not something ever done within my earshot.

During my childhood there were also several other important subjects that polite society felt it best to avoid (except when speaking discreetly, sotto voce). They included how much money you made, and any reference to your politics.

All these subjects were to be avoided. Being a polite boy I would never have broached the subject of religion with anyone in the family. But I observed, especially as a teenager, the tensions between my grandmother's participation in organized religion and her children's derisive remarks about religion and its practice. Wanting approval all around, I didn't know where I stood—and wouldn't for years.

Being for or against a particular issue—secular ones, of course—was the center of conversation at the dining table. But religion was omitted. Whether a person might be Roman Catholic or Jewish was occasionally mentioned. (That someone could be Jewish but not "observant" might be noted.) Yet I could observe the contrast between my grandparents and their children, meaning my mother and uncles, in their attitudes to religion. And this striking difference between the generations puzzled me.

One thing I understood from my grandmother: our faith was for everyday use, not simply Sunday attendance at a beautiful church. I felt this made sense, and indeed it became nothing less than the foundation of my identity and my values. I sensed that this profound belief also lay deep within my grandfather, even if we never talked about it.

My grandfather had no trouble referring to his religious values in his political speeches. Note the statement below that he made to a Democratic Party convention.

> Never since the early days of the New England town meeting have the affairs of Government been so widely discussed and so clearly appreciated. It has been brought home to us that the only effective guide for the safety of this most worldly of worlds, the greatest guide of all, is moral principle.
>
> We do not see faith, hope, and charity as unattainable ideals, but we use them as stout supports of a Nation fighting the fight for freedom in a modern civilization.
>
> Faith in the soundness of democracy in the midst of dictatorships.

Hope renewed because we know so well the progress we have made.

Charity in the true spirit of that grand old word.

For charity literally translated from the original means love, the love that understands, that does not merely share the wealth of the giver, but in true sympathy and wisdom helps men to help themselves.

We seek not merely to make Government a mechanical implement, but to give it the vibrant personal character that is the very embodiment of human charity.

We are poor indeed if this Nation cannot afford to lift from every recess of American life the dread fear of the unemployed that they are not needed in the world. We cannot afford to accumulate a deficit in the books of human fortitude.

Would you find either George Bush or Bill Clinton addressing their fellow Democrats or Republicans in this highly political way, while using faith, hope and charity as the basis for condemning the immorality of their political opposition?

But even though religion was not talked about, I grew up in a family where morality was very much the background to our lives. Even "spirituality" was not referenced—I suspect it would be considered too personal—but what was considered right, and what was wrong, was plainly drawn from a religious sense. There was nothing rigid—politics requires flexibility and compromise (even deviousness)—but the underlying morality based on religious conviction was always there.

9

Hostility of Eleanor Roosevelt toward Her Mother-in-Law

Eleanor Roosevelt is an icon who stands apart among the many celebrities of the twentieth century. More than just a celebrity, she was a political figure both as first lady and, after FDR's death, when she represented the United States at the United Nations. She continued to write her daily column, My Day. She also wrote regularly for magazines, published her autobiography, and appeared frequently on radio and television. In the last ten years of her life she wrote several books. With her overflowing diary of appointments she was seen as being always in perpetual motion.

During the White House years she had become loved by many Americans across the country—especially by women, because of her concern for them—owing to her compassion and her tireless energy as she worked to ease the pain of people suffering from the Great Depression and its aftermath. At the United Nations, more than any other delegate, she was the principal person behind the General Assembly's passing of the Universal Declaration of Human Rights in 1948. When she died, three presidents, Truman, Eisenhower, and Kennedy, as well as Vice President Lyndon Johnson, attended her funeral in the Rose Garden at our family house at Hyde Park, where she was buried next to her husband.

My grandmother was, and is, recognized as one of the

most influential people in the politics of her day. It is difficult to imagine anything said or written about her that would detract from her bright image. She is admired and revered all round the world. In his eulogy Adlai Stevenson even referred to her as "First Lady of the World." Thus, to consider that she might have had a dark side is akin to blasphemy.

Yet she did.

In my memoir of growing up in the White House under the tutelage of both my grandparents, Franklin and Eleanor, I am quite frank about the elements of Eleanor's personality that were a burden to me, particularly her persistent hostility toward my father. Her rigidity was practically ideological. But any criticisms I make in no way detract from my love and admiration for my grandmother. She was undoubtedly the most significant person shaping my life. But I feel it is important to make sure that those who greatly influence society—prominent figures in our history, such as Eleanor Roosevelt—are portrayed as fully human beings, many sided—just like the rest of us, and not just pictures in history books or statues cast in bronze, for us to look up to and admire. Pursuing that idea, I write this chapter because I have long been puzzled by my grandmother's having "taking against" her mother-in-law.

The fact is that Eleanor's hostility was largely responsible for sullying, indeed smearing, the image of Sara Delano Roosevelt, my great-grandmother. (As children, my sister and I her "Granny," just as our mother and her generation had done. As noted earlier in this book, we called our grandmother Eleanor "Grandmère.")

Sara Roosevelt indeed was a strong woman, an assured personality, confident of her secure place in society—and she enjoyed being the president's mother. She was one of the last of the Victorian grandes dames. She was also an excellent manager, working hard with her staff to maintain the family's estate at Hyde Park, which her son, my grandfather, Franklin Roosevelt, considered his home. Sublimely self-assured, Granny was the much-loved matriarchal figure for our family.

In retrospect it appears to me to be Granny's confident acceptance of her role in society— and in our family—that really bothered my grandmother. Granny would have smiled, much amused, at hearing herself referred to as a grande dame, but she wouldn't dream of changing her lifestyle. It was who she was.

But to disapprove of your mother-in-law's Victorian background and her calm acceptance of the upper-class position in which she was raised is not sufficient grounds for Eleanor's pointed hostility—what I call "taking against." Yet that is what Eleanor Roosevelt did, setting the pace in establishing a false image of Sara. And it was backed up by Eleanor's authorized biographer, Joseph Lash, in all of his books, as I will show later.

It is my grandmother's stereotyped portrayals that the press routinely echoes when describing Sara Roosevelt as dominating, bossy, and constantly interfering. Sara's son, Franklin, is frequently described as being "dominated" by his mother. Sara becomes a set piece, an arrogant and spiteful ogre, a mother-in-law who made Eleanor Roosevelt's life miserable. She is a throwback to an old order. Journalists, probably seeking facile characterizations, use adjectives such as snobbish, overbearing, bullying, and controlling when describing Sara Roosevelt's treatment of her daughter-in-law. Oh, poor Eleanor! Many times I heard my grandmother, with a rueful smile, regaling the company after supper with stories of her plight. She would describe her mother-in-law as totally out of step with today's world.

It was indeed she who launched this pattern of exaggerated images. Writing or speaking to family and close friends, the word got around: "Mrs. Roosevelt said . . ." You may read in the archives of the Roosevelt Library what my grandmother wrote to many people, including my mother. I quote some of these remarks in *Too Close to the Sun*. The widely read *McCall's* magazine printed what they said was an unpublished article by my grandmother—though it is now known to be a hoax—in which Eleanor is highly critical of Sara. For many years the U.S. Park Service unwittingly used this article as the background for their "interpretation" of Springwood for visitors. Fortunately, this has now been changed.

So I want to explore as best as I can what is behind all this. Eleanor's focused hostility toward Sara simply bears no relation to the kindness and toleration for which my grandmother is known. To me, it is more than puzzling. Particularly for those of us who lived with Eleanor Roosevelt and revere her, it is a profound contradiction.

A review of the history helps.

When Eleanor became engaged to marry Franklin Roosevelt she was, as I see it, very much a bundle of inhibitions, likely the reflection of the many conflicts carried forward from her difficult childhood. Women of her background (not very different from Sara's own) were taught to be self-assured, accustomed to life with servants and governesses, confident in their privileged role in society. Eleanor Roosevelt, however, was not actually like that. She could put on a good front, but underneath there was an *abîme* (an abyss) of anxiety.

From what my grandmother recalled of her own mother, it does not seem to me that Anna Hall Roosevelt encouraged confidence in her daughter. The child was not allowed to feel she could become like her mother. It is possible Eleanor was more at ease with her father; but how did she interpret his long absences—sent away from home to "recover" from his alcoholic and drug addictions? As an eight- or nine-year-old, did she guess at the truth? While it did not alter the sentimental love Eleanor always carried for her father, her relationship with him as a child certainly could not have encouraged her acquiring a sense of personal confidence. Further, my grandmother never mentioned enjoying a special relationship with either a nurse or a governess, with whom she would have spent a good amount of time.

Also, in contrast to her father, Eleanor could see the confidence exuded by his brother, her uncle Theodore Roosevelt. She admired his exuberant style, but "the vigorous life" he espoused scared her. She did not enjoy the paper chases at Sagamore Hill that his children reveled in. And, as Eleanor writes, her contacts with people of her own age were very restricted. In many ways she grew up alone. Her education was neglected—she was not taught to read until after the age of seven, and then only because an aunt intervened.

Certainly Eleanor Roosevelt was very well-mannered—you could see and feel the upper-class background within her—but she was also extremely shy. She was very different from Theodore Roosevelt's children, and from the Hall children on her mother's side of the family.[1] Not unlike Sara, these children accepted their privileged role in the society of that day, whereas Eleanor always seemed slightly apologetic about it.

People of the Victorian upper class were supposed to have both rights and duties. Most were more conscious of their privileged position and less of their duties. Eleanor emphasized the obligations. I was instructed by my grandmother to pay special attention to "those less fortunate than we are." Duty and obligation remained driving forces in Eleanor Roosevelt's life.

Beneath her well-mannered exterior, however, was an insecurity, which could not be hidden after she was married. In Sara's company she may well have been in awe of her always self-assured mother-in-law, but it is apparent from the exchange of letters at that time that Eleanor Roosevelt had hoped—desperately—that she would find in Sara someone to fill the gap her own mother had left in her psyche. But is that not asking a lot of your mother-in-law?

After marrying she turned to this new figure in her life with eager anticipation. The early letters between them show my grandmother overflowing with phrases of love, adoration, and devotion, calling Sara "Mummy."

"Thank you so much dear for everything you did for us. You are always the sweetest, dearest Mama to your children and I shall look forward to our next long evening together, when I shall want to be kissed all the time!" She signed, "Ever and ever so much love my dearest Mummy from your devoted Eleanor."[2]

Granny replied lovingly, in no way unwilling to offer personal attention to her new daughter-in-law. But Sara was, I would guess, perplexed by the expectations laid upon her by Eleanor. Granny had been raised with loving parents and had many siblings, all of whom were socially poised, well-trained to assume their responsibilities. The Warren Delanos were a close-knit family. Although typically paternalistic, they were loyal and loving kin—and confident!

Sara must have wondered at Eleanor's inadequacy when it came to fulfilling the usual responsibilities of a wife and mother from their background. Running a house with servants and (with nurses in tow) supervising the care of her children was the accepted routine. Yet Eleanor always backed off, saying she was afraid, that she "didn't know how." She further excused herself by adding that she had never played with dolls when a child.

She would later write: "For the first year of my married life, I was completely taken care of. My mother-in-law did everything for me." At the time, her own letters showed a deep gratitude for Sara's assumption of the simple chores that frightened her so inordinately. There was no indication that Eleanor resented her mother-in-law's help; indeed, she saw it for what it was intended to be—an expression of love.[3]

In contrast, Sara had gotten down on her knees and bend over the tub rim to bathe baby Franklin herself, the nurse standing to the side ready with a towel. Her daughter-in-law, on the other hand, let the hired nanny do everything, feeling that the nurse knew far better than she did.

Her husband's mother was, I expect, puzzled by Eleanor's hesitancy—almost a lack of maternal instinct—and some disapproval may have crept into her voice when giving advice to her daughter-in-law. However, Jan Pottker writes in her book *Sara and Eleanor*:

> Sara was either oblivious to or confused by Eleanor's hidden emotions. . . . Sara never referred to these issues in her comprehensive journal or in her many letters. Although she may not have understood her daughter-in-law—nor did Franklin—she continually offered love, helped with the children, and gave constant support to the family, including large chunks of her personal fortune.[4]

I find the last sentence a definite overstatement, though she regularly assisted with school fees, clothes, and special events such as journeys to Europe. In later years she did become rather extravagant when giving gifts to her grandchildren. But that's another story.

Leaving the financial interrelationship aside, there was also the fact that my grandparents often left their children at Hyde Park in their grandmother's care, and for weeks on end. Much as Eleanor later ignored such facts, her own and Franklin's many dependencies upon Sara are plain to discern in the letters exchanged at that time.

While Eleanor always wrote expressing her gratitude for this largesse, I believe that part of her may well have resented it. It makes me wonder if my grandmother didn't somehow perceive this perpetual dependence as an expression of her own inner weakness. Over the years this feeling may have grown and become the background for her accusing Sara of being domineering and taking over their domestic lives. "They were more my mother-in-law's children than mine," Eleanor often said in later years—apparently not recognizing how this reflected upon her.

Though acknowledging she didn't do well at raising her children, Eleanor typically blamed Granny, but not entirely.

She told Joe Lash, "It did not come naturally to me to understand little children or to enjoy them." But as Lash notes, when writing about my grandmother's trying to engage her children in games and other activities, "she was not easygoing in such matters. The moralist in her was always in command."[5] As Geoffrey Ward surmises: "Eleanor's real trouble lay within. Her own accounts of her children and their doings, both in the letters she wrote during their infancy and in her much later autobiographical writings, are singularly joyless. For her, young children seem to have been for the most part merely sources of further anxiety—fragile, undisciplined, [and] uncontrollable."[6]

Jan Pottker writes: "Eleanor was unhappy at what she saw as her mother-in-law's usurpation of her children, just as Sara may have been displeased by Eleanor's lack of steady involvement. . . . There seemed to be no middle ground for Eleanor between arguing with Sara, as she records, and abjectly pleading for forgiveness. As for Sara, she never put down any record of these crosscurrents either in her many letters or in her journal."[7] But I think "usurpation" is too strong a word. Granny may have spoken plainly when she found my mother and her brothers' behavior rude and offending, and Eleanor may well have taken offense at the criticism. But I don't consider this to be "taking over."

The financial dependency was two-edged. Even though Eleanor and Franklin together had reasonable incomes to support a very pleasant lifestyle, they always overspent, knowing that Sara would supplement their income whenever needed. I have the impression that my grandfather saw nothing wrong with this pattern, while my grandmother was both accepting of and, I think, secretly resentful of it—but not raising her voice to limit it, either. Knowing your extravagances would always be covered was the easy way out when you were too shy to challenge anything.

It is accurate to note Granny's overindulgence of her grandchildren. As my uncle James once wrote, he and his siblings found that the best way to get around their parents, when they were being denied anything they wanted, was to appeal to Granny. My mother said she felt guilty about this, but I never heard my uncles express any regrets, or gratitude.

But Uncle Jimmy fails to note that most of the discipline in their life as children came from their grandmother. Sara was plainspoken. She would not tolerate rudeness from her grandchildren; she expected them to be well mannered, especially in the presence of adults. Boisterous rivalry was their style, and that did not always go down well with their grandmother, who saw how incapable their mother was at disciplining them.

Eleanor moved from offering a measured reprimand to permissiveness, in fact, opting out, perhaps not knowing quite what to say or do, perhaps afraid of doing the wrong thing. Franklin was of little help. His view was that the children needed to get it out of their system. But I feel he was more often wishing to avoid confrontation with his wife.

Granny's candor about her grandchildren was expressed without rancor, but there was no misunderstanding her meaning. Unlike my grandmother, there was nothing pejorative in her reprimands. Sara's expressions of discipline were straightforward, but her open and consistent love for her grandchildren was apparent both to my mother and her brothers. They did not feel a burden had been laid on them in the same way they did when their mother would attempt to discipline them.

My uncles complained of the pained look that would come over their mother's face, expressing her implicit judgmental response to them. No doubt Eleanor loved her children, but expressing it directly was apparently an emotion she could not bring forth. She cared deeply about them, but her expressions of this were limited to "doing" practical things for them.[8]

When her children's disruptive behavior at the dining table brought rebukes from Sara, her daughter-in-law felt that the criticism was as much directed at herself as at the children. Perhaps some of it was, but even if the fracas was only about a minor infraction, Eleanor might leave the table in high dudgeon—choosing, as I see it, to make a scene.

Criticism within the family, even when only implied, was not something Eleanor could tolerate. It immediately provoked her dark moods, as she acknowledged. And yet she made a point of not paying attention to the abundant public criticism directed at her from congressmen and newspaper columnists!

Granny believed in good manners—she felt they made life pleasant—and believed the children should be taught them. I remember the ease with which I could accept my great-grandmother's discipline, especially with regard to my sloppy table manners. Faced with my mother and my grandmother's admonitions, I closed off, resenting it, always super-sensitive to their judgmental manner. They were not teaching me something, but rather seemed to be criticizing me as if I had done something wrong.

When Granny first visited my grandmother and grandfather in their new house in Washington in 1912, after Franklin had been appointed assistant secretary of the navy, Sara noted in her diary: "Dined at 1733 N Street. Moved chairs and tables and began to feel at home." From reading the correspondence it is clear that Granny did feel that Franklin and Eleanor were her children, and part of that intimacy evidently included rearranging their furniture.

So what could Eleanor Roosevelt do about it? After listening to my grandmother tell stories of how her mother-in-law interfered in her life, I have always thought that all Eleanor would have had to do would be to say quietly but firmly to Sara, "Mama, *please stop interfering*, especially on matters relating to the children." But she didn't—she couldn't. Instead, she remained resentfully silent. My grandmother's letters to my mother indicate that even in the White House years, when Granny would suggest something being done differently, the first lady was not able to ask her mother-in-law to please stop intervening in household matters.

My guess is that probably no more than a few years after Eleanor's marriage to Franklin, it was inevitable that mother-in-law and daughter-in-law would prove a disappointment to each other. But rather than acknowledging this and settling into a reasonable relationship—one that papered over disagreements in order to avert hostility—Eleanor's resentment seemed to intensify and become more pointed over the years.

By the time I came on the scene, 1930, my grandmother was in early middle age, but there still wasn't any mellowing. On the contrary, in the instinctive way that children have of understanding relationships, I knew—I could feel—that my grandmother and my great-grandmother were not at ease with each other. Even when it was politely stated, I could sense my grandmother's actual core attitude. However, although I lived for many weeks at a time at Hyde Park with Granny, she never gave any indication of a reciprocal hostility toward her daughter-in-law.

Although writing sympathetically to her mother, Eleanor's only daughter, my mother, carefully avoided taking sides. I knew from my mother's comments that she toed a thin line between the love and respect she felt for her grandmother, Granny, and her compulsion to seek her own mother's approval. But it was not until I began writing my book that I read this correspondence closely and saw clearly that my grandmother was quite open in her critical remarks against Granny, clearly taking against her mother-in-law. My mother, Anna, so much in need of her own mother's approval, went along with it.

Joseph Lash's biography notes that Eleanor admitted that the problem was partly her fault— for not speaking up, and for having allowed Sara to keep her "under her thumb." This puzzles me. Eleanor Roosevelt was a strong woman, determined, even willful. I never felt my grandmother was under her mother-in-law's thumb, not for one moment—indeed, not under anyone's thumb! Unfortunately I lacked the courage to speak up and ask my grandmother why she didn't speak plainly to Granny about her grievances.

But the point that puzzles me most is why in this situation one woman exceeded to such a degree the usual strain and resentment that often appears between daughter-in-law and mother-in-law, acting out so profoundly. "Taking against" an individual is a strong expression of hostility, one sharply focused on that other person. Especially when you consider the "good form" manners in which both women were groomed, this seems to me quite odd. Poor form! The ingrained good manners of both should have provided them with acceptable ways of expressing their differences—and keeping a respectful distance. But Eleanor chose to focus on the grievances she held onto, allowing her dark moods to prevail.

One noticeable truth I find when reviewing my grandmother's unsparing criticism of Sara is that how much she was, in fact, very much like her mother-in-law. As I have noted, there was no mistaking Eleanor Roosevelt's background. Indeed there was a charm to it—a trait I see as one element of her extraordinary popularity with the American public—just as there was with her husband. David McCullough writes about Sara in an issue of *Psychology Today* of March 1983: "She had standards, and she had the gift for making everybody want to measure up." Might not the same be said about her daughter-in-law?

Eleanor went out of her way to champion the rights of people deprived of their dignity or barred from employment due to race or class or creed. But in my observation, her manner always subtly revealed the noblesse oblige she had been taught to practice, the obligatory behavior of someone who came from a privileged background—the same background as Granny had. Although of different generations, my great-grandmother and my grandmother were thus cut from the same Victorian-style cloth, in terms of class status. Both were reared with the accepted dictum of behaving in a tolerant and measured way.

Nonetheless, Sara and Eleanor were entirely different in terms of self-confidence and emotional stability. Sara, my

Granny, had both. People remarked on her serenity. Eleanor had neither until she was well into middle age. Granny had always had a strong personal sense of identity. I don't think my grandmother firmly settled into any identity of her own until she became "Mrs. Roosevelt" in the White House. And even then she was unable to be normally assertive with her mother-in-law. She lived with her outrage—but was not above telling her friends of her ordeals with "Franklin's mother." With neither her children nor her mother-in-law was Eleanor capable of putting her foot down.

As a matter of principle, Eleanor Roosevelt made every effort to step beyond the class system and the condescension implied in the phrase "for those less fortunate than we are"—even though she used it herself. Her personal background could be seen in the quiet and dignified way she presented herself. She may have felt strongly about anyone taking his or her social position too seriously, but her own class origin was clearly evident to everyone. At the same time, I observed how my grandmother had neither friends nor even many acquaintances from her own class background, perhaps manifesting in this way her distancing herself from it.

My grandmother was very much in tune with the changing social scene in America but had not always felt as strongly about progressive social issues. For example, she hadn't been a suffragette. Most of her liberal inclinations developed into convictions when she was in her middle thirties. Although basically a tolerant person, Eleanor became outraged when she saw people being hurt, such as by racial segregation. She identified with them.

Sara Delano Roosevelt, on the other hand, was not passionate about social issues. This is not surprising, but unlike many people of her class she wasn't against the changes her daughter-in-law was writing and speaking about. Compared to the total engagement of Eleanor, Granny's life held but limited contacts outside her friends and "the people on the place," our Hyde Park estate. Yet, when called to participate more broadly, usually as the president's mother, she complied with enthusiasm.

After living in the White House but a short time, I knew well what the correct positions—attitudes, really—were for those of us living under Eleanor Roosevelt's wing. I sensed the rights and wrongs in my grandmother's portfolio, who we were for and who we were against. Yet I also plainly saw that in practice, in my life in the White House, the classless society was full of holes. Simply put, that wasn't the way that life was, at least for me. I knew very well who was above me and who was below me. One was polite and friendly to everyone—that was the accepted style—but the pecking order was ingrained in me through my everyday contacts.

This background regarding the tense relationship between Eleanor Roosevelt and her mother-in-law, Sara Delano Roosevelt, is useful; it needs to be absorbed, seen in the context of a long-past culture. The kind of pointed hostility that developed between them is not common, however. And my grandmother was largely responsible for it.

The critical question remains: What made Eleanor's attitude so strikingly different from the usual expressions of family tensions? What was behind her taking against Sara, often so vindictively? It makes no sense, especially since the younger woman was known for her sincerity and warmth toward other people.

One piece of the puzzle may include the range of Eleanor's activity. She reached out to the whole of America. As we have seen, "Mrs. Roosevelt" became a household name. On the other hand, Sara's scope was more restrained. She sought nothing more than to do her duty, as she saw it.

As first lady, Eleanor focused intensely on the events, and the people, with whom she was brought into contact through her engagements, her speeches and interviews, her writing, and her visits around the country. Each activity was connected with the social issues of the day. She did not purposely gather information for her husband, disliking the press dub-bing her the eyes and ears of the president. But she shared with him her observations and assessments of how people were coping with the Great Depression and how much they understood of what he was trying to do through the New Deal programs. He greatly valued her opinions and read the notes and letters she regularly sent him.

It would never have occurred to Sara to assume this role. Although she supported FDR's New Deal, and said so when asked, she did have her own way of seeing at least one of his programs. When the new Social Security Act had become law, an embarrassed Treasury Department official had to advise the president that his mother had not paid her social secu-rity taxes, and refused to do so, saying, "I can take care of my own!" FDR quietly paid it, and ordered the official not to let his mother know of his intercession.

Sara regularly worked with a number of voluntary organi-zations, and not only those of traditional concern to WASPS (White Anglo-Saxon Protestants). She consistently supported the Africa-America Institute and more than once hosted social events at her New York City house, including a fund raiser, in honor of Mary McLeod Bethune, the prominent African American leader. In 1938 the Jewish Forum awarded her the Albert Einstein Medal for Humanitarianism, noting Sara's "broad sympathy and activities in alleviating the conditions of all people throughout the world who suffer from poverty, oppression and hatred." In support of Eleanor, Sara invited to Hyde Park members of the Women's Trade Union League, including Eleanor's friend Rose Schneiderman.

I mention these engagements as representative of Sara's attitude, one not actually like what is usually reported. Elea-nor's later comments about her mother-in-law would some-times lead you to believe that Sara's interests were limited to sewing circles and traditional (safe) charities. One of Sara's regular activities did include teaching a new system of sew-ing at the school in Hyde Park village, and she sewed clothes for dolls to be given to hospitalized children. Additionally, there were the usual organizations such as the Red Cross, or other church-related charities. New York City's Greenwich House, founded to help the local immigrant community, was one of Sara's special interests.

Unlike many of her class, Sara was not anti-Semitic. She was a supporter of B'rith Abraham and Hadassah, once traveling to Toronto to address their group. When my great-grandmother died, a spokeswoman for the Young Women's Zionist Organization of America said, "Her [Sara's] understanding of the problems of minority groups and her sympathies with their aims endeared her to Americans of all faiths."

At one Mother's Day celebration, Sara spoke in the address she gave of her concern for "the great multitude—many millions—of homeless mothers, war orphans, impoverished refugees. . . . This we shall do without neglecting the needy of our own land." Eleanor remarked in her column: "There is no one I know who sets a greater value on the duties and pleasures of motherhood." Considering all Sara's other activities, I hear this as a rather sly remark on Eleanor's part, relegating her mother-in-law to "motherhood."[9]

One basic difficulty in penetrating into why Eleanor Roosevelt took against her mother-in-law is that Eleanor so soon turned into an icon after becoming first lady in the White House. When I grew up, indeed throughout most of my life, anything my grandmother said was, I felt, undoubtedly true. She was one of those people whose integrity was not questioned. So when she spoke and wrote about Sara Delano Roosevelt, particularly after Franklin had died, in ways that created the now widely accepted image of Sara as an arrogant and out-of-touch woman with a controlling nature, this version became the whole truth and nothing but the truth.

Although known across America as a model of tolerance and respect for the rights of all people, perhaps it is now possible to say out loud: Hold on. Eleanor did have a dark side, and she did engage in hostility toward a selected few. This perhaps means she was only human as well as humane.

Perhaps more than by anyone else, Eleanor's disparaging public images of Sara Delano Roosevelt were nailed firmly in place by Joseph P. Lash, my grandmother's authorized biographer. In his best-selling book entitled *Eleanor and Franklin*, he writes: "She [Sara] was a matriarch who belonged completely to a past generation; she sought to dominate . . . from behind a facade of total generosity, submission and love." False characterizations such as the above occur throughout, and he regularly slips in the snide word or phrase to reinforce his own derogative views. Lash writes: "She [Eleanor] had to bear the brunt of Sara's harassment and discontent."[10] He drags in my eighteen-year-old mother when he writes: "Alone with her grandmother [Anna] had to bear the brunt of Sara's harassment and discontent." In fact, I know from my mother that, being regularly at odds with her own mother, she often would seek out her grandmother, Sara, as her confidante.

In *Eleanor and Franklin*, Lash, too, describes how Sara stepped in with financial assistance when it was needed. He records at one point, my grandmother's anxiety about unpaid bills piling up. "There were large doctors' bills that spring, between Johnny's knee and Brother's broken nose and Elliott's rupture and James digestive troubles." He then notes: "Sara as usual came to the rescue," at the same time noting the relief expressed by Eleanor at her mother-in-law's help.[11] None of this sounds at all as though Sara's generosity was greatly resented.

Another example from Lash's biography of Eleanor is the funny but sad story that follows.[12] Lash notes that FDR was spending most of his time concentrating on trying to recover from polio. Hence my grandmother was planning a European trip with her two close friends, Marion and Nancy, taking along her two youngest children, Franklin Jr. and Johnnie: "It was also Sara who a month later almost undid the European trip during a family dinner at the Big House. Eleanor was reviewing their plans for the trip—they were taking the Buick and Chevy and she, Nan, and Marion would do the driving; perhaps they might even do some camping. Suddenly Sara reared up, disapprovingly—it would be undignified for the wife of the governor and two of his sons to motor in an old touring car and even worse for the governor's wife to drive herself."

Hearing this, "Eleanor then turned to the head of the table where Sara always sat opposite Franklin, and said in a cold voice, 'Very well. I will take your grandsons in a manner consistent with what you think their positions ought to be.'" With that she hurried out of the dining room and took refuge on the screened porch."

Lash concludes:

But Franklin did not contradict Sara. She again had her way, and the incident cast a shadow over the entire trip. . . . Eleanor rented handsome chauffeur-driven limousines everywhere they went, beginning with a Daimler in England, and made the boys sit in the back with her, although they longed to sit up front with the driver.

I heard this story several times from my grandmother, so I know from whence Lash obtained it. But note the phrase he uses to describe Sara's response to Eleanor's plans: "Suddenly Sara reared up, disapprovingly." That's simply his interpretation. "Rearing up" was not something Sara would do; it would be poor form, bad manners, something quite unnecessary for someone with Sara's self-confidence. She was not expressing anger, only an outdated sense of propriety.

For my part, I feel this characterization of my great-grandmother reflects the author's lack of understanding of upper-class routines of the time—such as the normality of having a chauffeur drive your car. (In New York City, in 1936, I was regularly driven to school by one.) Granny's somewhat outdated notion of the dignity that should be accorded to the governor's wife and sons might well have been dismissed by one of FDR's "amusing remarks," and the whole scene would have been laughed off—if only my grandmother had not decided to make a scene. And about what? I have always wondered whom it was she was punishing.

What I don't understand, considering his long friendship with Eleanor, and the fact that he was a professional writer, is how Lash could ignore the imprint on her of her very distinct background. In his biography he quite misses this basic element of her personality. She was reared in the same class as her mother-in-law, and it was evident all her life. Eleanor was well-known for her liberal views but her demeanor was always revealing.

Joe Lash was a professional writer, a prober of events, long before he became Eleanor's biographer. But he refused to entertain the possibility that Eleanor was rationalizing her feelings of inadequacy, attempting to justify what she considered to be her failures as a mother. "I never played with dolls when I was a child" was an oft-repeated excuse of my grandmother's, one that made me cringe. Lash writes that Eleanor felt that "if she had insisted on caring for her own children . . . she as well as they would have been happier." Elsewhere in his book he acknowledges (as does Eleanor in her autobiography) that she was simply incapable of giving to her children the love they so much wanted. Lash quotes Eleanor: "I was certainly not an ideal mother. . . . It did not come naturally to me to understand little children or to enjoy them. Playing with children was difficult for me because play had not been an important part of my childhood."[13]

Joe knew all my uncles and thought them loud and arrogant, indeed confirming Granny's characterization of them as not being well brought up, but he makes no comment on my grandmother's excuses. Like me he regularly heard her offering these same explanations for her feeling that she didn't do well with children.

Perhaps Joe's intense loyalty to Eleanor also blocks him

from seeing that a sense of humor was not one of her strong points (nor of his, I should add). Additionally, it was known to all of us that Eleanor was likely to take immediate offence when she felt criticized. But Joe doesn't mention this; he doesn't relate it to the tensions between Eleanor and Sara.

In retrospect I can see that my great-grandmother was one of the last of a specific milieu, people who still had enough money to sustain themselves in their class position. Indeed Granny disdained those who did not know how to "handle money well" or those of her peers in society who did not practice the charitable responsibilities Granny felt were obligatory for a person graced with being "the well to do."

Sara Delano Roosevelt died in 1941, a month before the Pearl Harbor attack plunged us into World War II. I doubt that she would have found it easy to cope with a postwar America in which her world, the old order, made orderly by the class system, was well on its way out, no longer having the same role or carrying the same influence in our society.

I should note here my own glaring omission as of this point. I have not noted my grandfather's reaction to this open hostility that his wife expressed toward his mother. Of course he was aware of it. Eleanor would write to him about the exchanges she had had with Mama and how she had apologized the following day. FDR was sympathetic but careful not to take sides. He disliked an atmosphere of discord, especially when it was laced with his wife's anger. One reason, I presume, that FDR went to Florida, where he had rented a houseboat, was to escape the disturbing vibrations at home. He knew there was nothing he could say that would reduce the tension. Any intervention on his part would only make things more difficult.

The practice of taking against another person, with its pointed hostility, is a very neurotic trait. Unfortunately it is a well-known phenomenon, a most destructive prejudice when directed against a group or institution—Jews, Roman Catholics, Muslims, fundamentalists, people of nations we consider a threat, etc. From there it can be picked up and used by demagogues such as Adolf Hitler and propagated throughout a nation, or, to be more up to date, through the mass media. Likewise, indirectly, prejudice may be exploited for raising immense amounts of lobbying money to be used for narrow political ends.

Eleanor Roosevelt would be dismayed to find herself in this company. And it would be a gross injustice to place her there. What I wish to write about here is a blip in her personality, albeit a serious one. When one considers how much of a struggle it was for her to emerge from her inner turmoil and begin to open up, it is all the more strange to see her slip into such pointed hostility. Her choice of focus for her hostility makes it doubly puzzling. Sara certainly did not deserve to be taken against with such intensity. I do wonder why my grandmother felt such a strong need to do so—flying in the face of the very values such as understanding and compassion she had come to champion.

My object in this chapter has certainly not been to denigrate this woman I knew so well. It is to show that a person recognized as having extraordinary character—one whom we look up to, whose image for courage and sincerity has rightfully made her an icon of integrity—is still a human being, just like you and me. It may push her a bit off her pedestal, but what I describe in no way diminishes her greatness, nor my reverence for my grandmother.

However, I do not excuse my grandmother's biographer, whose judgment and lack of perspective I find glaring. He never probes the questions I raise above, rather obvious ones. Worse, few have challenged his unkind assertions about Sara Delano Roosevelt nor his unquestioned channeling of Eleanor's complaints.

I have maintained that Eleanor was very disappointed in not finding in FDR's mother the maternal figure she so desperately wanted. Was she also resentful at having been lumbered with child after child (six in all)—"always either pregnant or recovering from giving birth"—for so many years? Or—and this is highly speculative—was Eleanor's hostility toward Sara really a substitute for resentments against her husband? Any disappointment in Franklin may have seemed an expression of hostility that "a good wife" could not make openly. It is anybody's guess.

Eleanor's own writing gives us few leads, though I have cited her difficult childhood and lack of confidence. We also know that when confronted by behavior she felt to be oppressive, she could, as she said, turn "cold." Her close friend Nancy Cook has commented, "Eleanor can be very hard."

Eleanor herself writes plainly about her foul moods, and how she took out it on the people surrounding her. Even on her honeymoon there was an incident in which she "had lapsed into an irritable and aggrieved silence—a pattern of behavior that would be repeated hundreds of times in the years to come."[14] Many people live with their hostility repressed inside them. My grandmother did so most of the time, but occasionally she let it out and, in my observation, she then produced an object of hostility that was not at all realistic. She created the hostile image to suit her needs, one such as her mother-in-law. Even Sara's death did not alter my grandmother's attitude. In fact my grandmother went right on telling the same stories of how difficult a person Franklin's mother had been and what a burden.

In a letter reporting to my mother about Granny's funeral, Eleanor wrote of Sara, "I kept being appalled at myself because I couldn't feel any real grief or sense of loss & that seemed terrible after 36 years of fairly close association."[15]

While I admire my grandmother's candor, her admission makes me very sad.

1. Franklin and Eleanor
Roosevelt, the young couple.

2. My grandmother and grandfather are
older here. In the background is the
covered walkway of the White House.

3. My mother, Anna, is typing a letter home from her room in Livadia Palace during the Yalta Conference, February 5, 1945.

4. Anna is here with Kathy Harriman, who is translating a Soviet anti-Franco propaganda billboard in Yalta, February 10, 1945.

5. FDR and Anna greeting
Emperor Haile Selassie and the
Crown Prince of Ethiopia.

6. My great-grandmother, Sara Delano
Roosevelt, with her only child, her
son, Franklin D. Roosevelt.

7. A family picture posed on the
front portico of our house at Hyde
Park, in 1932. I am on my mother's
lap with my father standing behind
her. I would be two years old.

8. All of us grandchildren, at our grandfather's inauguration in January of 1945. This picture is taken in his study on the second floor of the white House. I am in my military school uniform.

10

Others in the White House Entourage

My life in the White House and at Hyde Park was filled with interesting people. Books have been written about some of them—Louis Howe and Harry Hopkins, for example. Others, such as Marion Dickerman, have written their own memories.

I think one should have been written about my Cousin Polly, Miss Laura Delano. She was a character, both looking and acting the part well. Petite, rustling about in silk pajamas, (which she donned for the evening), she covered her hands and wrists with rings and bracelets that all tinkled and clattered when she gesticulated as she talked.

All this was topped by a rather haughty face, defined by a high forehead. Her hair was dyed either blue or mauve, perhaps a shade in between. The total effect was one of amazing grace and style.

Yet it seemed quite casual. Polly displayed such charm when entering a room that all were riveted. She liked to gossip and always had a juicy story for Cousin Franklin. (She chose to avoid the nasty cutting style of Alice Roosevelt, a cousin from the Teddy Roosevelt branch of the family.)

Cousin Polly (or Cousin Laura, as we called her when we were children) was a favorite of my grandfather, and was with him in Warm Springs when he died. As I have learned more about my great-grandmother's family, the Delanos,

Polly doesn't seem to fit in with their style. Obviously she had cut away from their norm and established herself with a distinct personality.

During World War I, when my grandparents were living in Washington due to FDR's post as assistant secretary of the navy, Laura Delano was also there. She created a real scandal—within a very limited circle, as it was so scandalous!—by falling head over heels in love with the first secretary of the Japanese embassy. For many Americans at the time, prejudice against Asian peoples was not far different from their prejudice against African Americans. It didn't matter that Cousin Polly's love was a prince in the Japanese royal family. But there was more. They wanted to get married! It was his family that put its foot down. The prince must marry someone more appropriate for his station, said his parents. I was told that Cousin Laura had been devastated and remained "Miss Delano" henceforth.

But the story picks up again at the beginning of World War II, when Eleanor Roosevelt's secretary received a request from a man at the head of the Japanese mission sent from Tokyo to discuss peace with the United States. The gentleman was requesting to take tea with the first lady. Eleanor's secretary was naturally startled, but my grandmother recognized the name immediately. It was Cousin Polly's sweetheart from World War I. So she had tea—tête à tête—and unknown to the press, with the prince. She told me he couldn't have been more gracious and asked, please, to be remembered to Miss Delano.

Cousin Polly had a lovely house about twenty minutes' drive north of our home at Hyde Park. It was close enough for FDR to drive himself there in his little blue convertible, and he usually went at teatime. He didn't drink and then drive since shifting, steering, and braking all needed to be done by hand in his specially designed car.

When Winston Churchill was visiting Hyde Park during World War II, FDR drove the two of them to visit Miss Delano in the late afternoon. They sat outside on her lovely flagstone terrace. FDR accepted tea. The prime minister wanted a whiskey. Out came both the tea tray and the drinks tray. Cousin Polly, puffed up a little perhaps by this visitation from two heads of government, decided to make Mr. Churchill one of the dark rum cocktails for which she was famous. It was a simple concoction—a large slug of Myers's dark Jamaican rum with just enough lemon juice and sugar added to hide the strong taste of the alcohol. (They were marvelous, and I can report that just one of them made me quite tiddly.)

She handed the prime minister his drink and turned to pour FDR his tea. Churchill, in the midst of telling a story, took it in his hand without noticing that it wasn't his whiskey, and took a first sip. He immediately spat it out on the flagstones. "This isn't whiskey!" he roared. FDR, watching the whole scene, couldn't help but laugh.

One of my earliest memories of the people in my "extended family," all living in the White House and present at mealtimes, is that of Louis Howe. I had no idea how important he had been in my grandfather's ascendance to the presidency. But I certainly was aware of his formidableness. Obviously, he was an important person. From the moment I entered the room, and would dutifully peck him on the cheek—he was entitled to that—I kept my distance. Occasionally, when very young, I was plopped in his lap. As I've written, to this day I can recall the scent of his cigarettes. They were pungent and his clothes reeked of them. The smell of the dangling cigarette being presently smoked was fine, I liked it; it was its predecessors that made me wrinkle my nose. (Secondary smoke inhalation was not a consideration in those days; everyone smoked, except for Granny and my grandmother.)

When you were as close to Mr. Howe as I so often was, sitting on his lap, I understood why Granny, always with her voice lowered, let drop that she regarded him as none too clean. "Dirty" was the word she used. From being within inches of his pockmarked face with its sallow skin, I could have confirmed to her that he did have a body odor. But I would have had to add that it blended well with the Sweet Caporal cigarettes, a not unpleasant staleness that went with the fallen cigarette ashes regularly decorating his waistcoat and shirtfront.

Granny had several reservations about Louis Howe, especially when it came to having him "at table": for one, he was a journalist. A trade, not a profession, she said. His gruff manner, gravelly voice, and the rumpled look of his clothes didn't endear him to her either. What's more, that he smoked and drank with her son was something Granny could not approve of. But he was her son's *éminence grise*, and so that was that.

FDR's solid and long-standing rapport with Howe was plain for Granny—for all of us—to see and feel. So she went along with her son's choice of confidant, as well as with the other odd characters FDR brought to the table, persons that would not ordinarily have graced her home with their presence (Senator Huey Long, for example).

Eleanor Roosevelt, too, had developed a strong rapport with Louis Howe, but not before first going through a long period when she shared some of Granny's reservations. Now I watched her ask him questions—what he thought about this or that—whenever she joined the company. Even as first lady she was clearly somewhat in awe of Louis Howe's knowledge of and instinct for the political world.

My own response to Mr. Howe was to take in all the others' reactions. Thinking and feeling for myself was of secondary importance to absorbing cues, usually from my maternal authorities. Therefore, Louis Howe was always "Mr. Howe" to Sis and me—and also to Granny.

The presence of Aunt Marion Dickerman and Aunt Nancy Cook at Hyde Park are part of my earliest memories, and also some of my later ones. They were such close friends of my grandmother's that they shared a house, the Stone Cottage, about a mile and a half east of the Big House on the Hudson

River, and just down the hill from my grandfather's retreat, Top Cottage. (All are now national historic sites.)

Aunt Marion got my grandmother quite interested in her school, the Todhunter School for Girls, in mid-Manhattan. And Eleanor was for a brief time its associate principal. My grandmother's pleasure in this involvement was one of the reasons she had initially resisted going to Washington to become first lady as the wife of the president.

By the time I was old enough to really notice, the relationship had soured enough for my grandmother to have built her own house adjacent to the Stone Cottage. Both are now referred to as Val-Kill. Still, the relationship between Eleanor, Aunt Marion, and Aunt Nancy remained sufficiently intact for my grandmother to ask Nancy to supervise completion of my summer school assignment in 1937.

Neither woman had been asked to join the government when FDR took office for the first time. Later, in the mid-1930s, when my grandmother was firmly established as the iconic Mrs. Roosevelt, these two old friends seemed to want to take some of the credit for her public transformation. Eleanor was quite shocked and even incensed. She finally bought out her former companions, at which juncture she owned the whole property of Val-Kill.

Throughout all this period of injured feelings my grandfather continued to see that Sara invited them to supper whenever he was at Hyde Park. He liked their company; they could talk politics. Nancy had been a staff member at the New York Democratic Party headquarters and Marion had been on the campaign trail with my grandmother.

The last time I saw Aunt Nancy (it was probably in the late 1950s) was when she had invited my grandmother to be the speaker at a women's gathering close to her home. The two of them were very kind and complimentary to each other.

Years later, when researching material for my book, I spent an afternoon with Aunt Marion in her Connecticut home (Nancy had died). She couldn't have been nicer, although most of her remarks were about my grandfather. But there was nothing nasty said about my grandmother. In her autobiography she gives the strong impression that it was FDR with whom she was really close. So much for memory!

The woman known by all as Missy was one of my second grandmothers. Marguerite LeHand had been FDR's secretary during his campaign in 1920 for the vice presidency and stayed with him after the campaign when he joined an insurance firm in order to earn a living and support his family. She was with him a great deal during the eight-year period when my grandfather devoted himself to his recovery efforts from the crippling polio. Then she resumed working for him full time after he was elected governor of New York. When he entered the White House, she occupied the housekeeper's small suite there on the third floor. Missy was the only name I ever heard used when referring to her. According to my mother, she was simply part of the family, an addition to its core group since the early 1920s.

Missy was obviously a lasting favorite of my grandfather. She had a rapport with him second to none. Some historians consider her to have been as influential with FDR as Harry Hopkins was. Supreme Court Justice Felix Frankfurter recalled: " She was one of the very few people who was not a 'yes-man' . . . she told the president not what she knew he wanted to hear, but what were, in fact, her true views and convictions."[1] Harry Hopkins recalls often having lunch with FDR and Missy at his desk.

There has been much gossip that she and FDR were having an affair. How stupid! She not only had her own rooms in the White House but also at Hyde Park, the family's home. FDR was rarely alone with anyone but briefly, except in the Oval Office. With the constant presence of servants and Secret Service men, Missy's movements were as well monitored as the president's.

Somehow Missy understood how to enter into a friendship with my grandmother, and Eleanor would be the first to acknowledge her as being part of the family. Even with the obvious closeness Missy had with FDR—so clearly visible at the cocktail hour, for example—my grandmother understood that they were not having an affair.

However, twenty years of long hours, being on call twenty-four hours a day, would take its toll on her. In the spring of 1941 she had first a minor stroke and then a massive one that left one side paralyzed. Within a few months she died. FDR grieved. She had always, it seemed, been there beside him—and not only as an adviser but as his close friend. With my grandfather's power of attorney she wrote his checks and handled many of his personal affairs. To call her irreplaceable would be an understatement.

"Tommy," Malvina Thompson, was my grandmother's secretary. For me, perhaps even more than Missy, she seemed a second grandmother. She was already working for Eleanor when I came to live in the White House at the age of three. Her office was a tiny space at the back of the stairwell. But it was close to my grandmother's grand sitting room where she had her desk in a corner and books piled all around.

During our first Christmas at the White House, I hadn't known—I was too young, of course—that Tommy was going through a divorce, and that it wasn't easy. That Christmas Eve she attended church with my grandmother; afterward they went back to Tommy's apartment to celebrate briefly and open presents. Then my grandmother returned to the White House to follow her usual routine of preparing the contents of our Christmas stockings soon to be placed in front of the fireplace in our grandfather's bedroom. Eleanor greatly appreciated Tommy and their affection was mutual. But Tommy never called my grandmother anything but Mrs. Roosevelt. Their relationship was of a different sort than the one Missy LeHand enjoyed with FDR; both, though, were important ones.

Sometimes Tommy had other duties, ones quite unusual for a secretary. When I was in first grade at Buckley in New York City, we presented our end-of-term play, just before Christmas. My mother was in Seattle and my grandmother was traveling, so it was Tommy who attended in loco parentis, seeing me as the drummer boy. In no way did I feel neglected; she was one of my extra grandmothers and it seemed quite natural to me for her to be the one to attend my performance.

Later, when Sis and I returned to the White House as teenagers, we would always join our mother in going straight to Tommy upon arrival. We wanted to find out what was happening, who would be visiting, and any hot gossip that might be circulating. With all the people piling in to ask Tommy questions, it was amazing that she got any of my grandmother's work done. Tommy always traveled with my grandmother, wrote her checks, kept her in cash, and was used to taking dictation on her lap while riding in a swaying train or a noisy airplane.

When my grandmother built her own cottage at Val-Kill, she included an apartment for Tommy—living room, kitchen, guest room (Tommy had a close friend, Henry Osthagen, who often visited on weekends), as well as Tommy's bedroom. My grandmother often used Tommy's guest room for her own guests—but only after first asking Tommy whether Henry was coming that weekend. During the day family members would drop by to catch up on the gossip with Tommy. And it was in Tommy's sitting room that the family gathered for cocktails every evening, using her kitchen as the bar where all the liquor was kept. Tommy didn't seem to mind all of these intrusions. Actually, I feel she enjoyed being at the hub of the family.

When I accompanied my grandmother to Europe in the autumn of 1948 for the meeting of the United Nations' General Assembly, Tommy and I became companions. I was recovering from an illness and was on "limited duty." If I wasn't organizing the guests for lunch or supper for my grandmother, Tommy and I would eat together. And we always had a drink together before her boss came home to the Hôtel de Crillon. (Tommy kept a bottle of Scotch in her desk drawer.)

In Paris, however, Tommy was beginning to show her age and did not accompany my grandmother to the same extent to which she had been accustomed previously. By this time Eleanor had a second secretary, Maureen Corr, who began to substitute for Tommy on my grandmother's journeys. And there'd be times when Tommy had had a bit too much to drink to be able to take dictation at 9:00 p.m. (Yes, just like Missy, Tommy was on call twenty-four hours a day.) But Tommy was family, and there was no thought of moving her out. Val-Kill was her home. When she died I did sense my grandmother was rather relieved. But life would not be the same without Tommy, not for Eleanor nor for the family.

A vignette: One time at Val-Kill, when my grandmother and I were sitting alone, I had the temerity to ask her what Tommy was paid. When my grandmother told me, I replied that that was much less than my secretary was paid. My grandmother replied defensively that Tommy had no expenses. So I asked what she would live on if Eleanor died. My grandmother nodded and I knew she had taken my point. Soon after, I learned that Tommy was to receive the proceeds from my grandmother's latest book. Then shortly afterward, Tommy died, so it was her niece who benefited.

My mother, sister, and I all mourned Tommy's demise. Val-Kill was different without her. My grandmother, who always used the desk in her bedroom—a very cramped arrangement— moved over to Tommy's desk in the corner of her sitting room. But we continued to use the room, too, for the family cocktail hour, and always referred to it as "Tommy's room." Still, without her it wasn't quite the same.

My uncles would also occasionally be in residence when they were home from school or college. They were the darlings of my great-grandmother. (My sister and I were also.) My father told me this story many years later: Granny had given James, my oldest uncle, a ticket to Europe and a substantial sum of money to spend during his vacation there. Jimmy thought he would need more money so he asked my father, Curtis Dall, then a stockbroker, about doubling the amount through a quick deal on Wall Street. Dad said it could be done, but that he also risked losing everything. Jimmy was willing, and he lost all his cash. The next morning at the breakfast table my grandmother said to my father "I understand, Curt, that you have lost all of Jimmy's money. Don't you think you should pay him back?" According to my father, he replied simply, "Yes, Mama." Dad said he had to borrow the money to do so. But good form was maintained, and Jimmy went off to Europe.

John Steinbeck came to see the president during the height of the Battle of Britain when England had its back to the wall. The well-known author's suggestion for winning the war against the Nazis was less than helpful. But it had pricked FDR's humor, his enjoyment of something outlandish. Steinbeck had suggested flooding Germany with counterfeit bills, thereby breaking the back of their economy, and bringing the nation down to defeat.

Rather than saying no directly, not something FDR liked to do, he instead sent Steinbeck over to see the secretary of the treasury, Henry Morgenthau Jr., whose department had under its wing the Secret Service. Part of the job of the Secret Service, in addition to protecting the president, was to deal with the bogus duplication of the bills printed by the U.S Treasury. Also, and this is really the point of the story, FDR knew his old friend had a puritanical streak unleavened by a sense of humor. And my grandfather could anticipate the secretary's response.

The Morgenthaus were family friends whom my sister and I referred to as "Uncle Henry" and "Aunt Elinor." They often joined us at supper and did so after the Steinbeck visit. While FDR already knew of the secretary's reaction he decided to twit him about it. "I understand, Henry, that you're not keen on John Steinbeck's suggestion for winning the war." Up rose Uncle Henry from his soup to protest. "Franklin! My department does not engage in counterfeiting!"

Actually, I don't remember his exact words, but I do remember his splutter and righteous indignation while most of the company fell about laughing, including FDR.

Over the years I have heard all manner of criticisms of my grandfather and grandmother. But one, repeated quite often, was especially disturbing to me. This is because I felt the implied anti-Semitism behind the remark: "FDR had a lot of Jewish advisers and Eleanor Roosevelt had a lot of Jewish friends." In both instances, the strong implication was "too many."

I had known Judge Samuel Rosenman for as long as I can remember. A frequent guest at our meals, he was FDR's main speechwriter for seventeen years, beginning when my grandfather was governor of New York State. A book about his experiences, *Presidential Style: Some Giants and a Pygmy in the White House*, was finished by his wife, Dorothy, and published after his 1973 death. But an earlier memoir by him, published in 1952, bore the simpler title *Working with Roosevelt*. And that he certainly did.

The Moranthaus—Henry, his wife, Elinor, and their children—were significant family friends. If we were at Hyde Park they would be at supper or at least attending the cocktail hour, their place in Fishkill being only a short drive from us. It may seem odd now, but as a child I was surprised to discover that Uncle Henry was in the government—in the Department of Agriculture—and then I was quite bowled over to learn later that my grandfather had appointed him as secretary of the treasury. I was impressed.

Their children, Joan, Robert (Bob), and Henry III, were more my mother and uncles' generation but I did become friendly with Henry III when living as a young adult in New York. Joan went on to become a doctor and I saw little of her. Bob had a brilliant war record, including having his ship torpedoed under him and spending days in a small life raft before being rescued. Later he became district attorney of

New York and was elected over and over again, not retiring until he was about ninety years old.

But during my childhood, living in the White House, I knew only that Aunt Elinor was a very close friend of my grandmother. They regularly rode horseback together and she was one of the very few people who called "Mrs. Roosevelt" Eleanor. My grandmother really grieved when she died in August 1949.

Uncle Henry and Aunt Elinor couldn't have been more different from each other. He always had a nice word for me and was enjoyable to be with. She was dour, with a stern face, apparently having serious things on her mind most of the time. She and my grandmother regularly discussed the issues of the day.

As I've mentioned, Uncle Henry had a rather limited sense of humor, which allowed my grandfather to have fun with him. But even when FDR would tease him relentlessly, he took it well. However, during cabinet meetings they would share scribbled cryptic comments about other cabinet members, such as sly remarks about Mrs. Perkins's new hat (or her rather big feet!), or one of the others sitting there who would take too long in making a point.

When I went to the just-established State of Israel in the autumn of 1948, my grandmother put me under the protective wing of Uncle Henry. (I've written a separate essay about this trip, "Eyewitness in Israel: 1948," and chapter 13 of this book describes the experience as well. I was an extraordinary adventure for an eighteen-year-old.) Henry Morgenthau was the new chairman of the United Jewish Appeal, the organization founded the year before to raise money in America to help support the new country, not yet six months old. Uncle Henry and several other U.S. Jewish leaders were making their first visit there, with Israel had providing the plane, the first craft for the new airline El Al. (It was a clapped-out DC4 that had been bought from surplus, the pilot told me.) I was on my own as a guest of the Israeli government, although Uncle Henry did take me to meet Prime Minister David Ben-Gurion before I left to rejoin my grandmother in Paris. Not my chaperone exactly—I was making trips around the country with escorts provided by the Israelis—he nonetheless felt a responsibility for me there.

After my grandfather died, I saw Uncle Henry only when I was visiting my grandmother at Val-Kill. He had a new wife, a Frenchwoman, Marcelle Puthon Hirsch, quite different from my Aunt Elinor. What I remember most about Marcelle were the extraordinarily thick glasses she wore owing to her very poor eyesight. Uncle Henry adored her.

Margaret Suckley, better known as Cousin Daisy, may well have been my grandfather's favorite lady after Missy LeHand died. She was with him in Warm Springs, along with Cousin Polly and Lucy Mercer (and Elizabeth Shoumatoff, who was painting the president's portrait) when he died on April 12, 1945. And she usually accompanied him when he went to the Top Cottage.

The family saw her as FDR's "gofer." As my grandmother put it, she was grateful to Cousin Daisy for keeping Franklin company during his brief but frequent visits to Hyde Park. She fetched this and that, picked up his pencil when it dropped and rolled out of his reach, and she pushed him in his wheelchair when he needed to be moved.

What we didn't notice was the intimate sympathy between the two of them. The fact of it was not brought clearly into the light until Geoffrey Ward edited the exchange of letters between them, found in her possession after her death in 1991, aged ninety-nine. Ward's book, titled *Closest Companion: The Unknown Story of the Intimate Friendship Between Franklin Roosevelt and Margaret Suckley*, was published in 1995. Sadly, and stupidly, a film later was made (the script originally had been a radio play on the BBC), and I was invited to a private screening in London, Here is my review:

The film *Hyde Park on Hudson* may not make as much money for its producers as they expected, considering the awful reviews they have had from the critics. Just desserts, I feel. After viewing the film it was obvious to me that making money must have been its sole objective.

Even if not a big box-office success it reveals what an appetite we have for sex—and *what disregard* we have for historical accuracy. Historical novels, plays, and cinema are my favorites. But there has to be some reasonable engagement with real history behind them. This film has none.

11

The Chaste Eleanor Roosevelt

After four years as governor of New York State, FDR moved from Albany to Washington and took up the residency he had always wanted—the White House. Contemplating being first lady, my grandmother was not all that pleased: quite dismayed, in fact. She had had firsthand observations of the dutifully prescribed roles of Mrs. Theodore Roosevelt and Mrs. Woodrow Wilson. What she wondered was whether she would be able to be more than a hostess, free to move beyond her White House social obligations.

Soon she had help formulating an answer. Lorena Hickok, a seasoned reporter assigned by the Associated Press to cover the new first lady, entered Eleanor's life and quickly become instrumental in the making of her new identity as "Mrs. Roosevelt." First off, Hickok suggested Eleanor begin holding her own press conferences, and for women reporters only—in sharp contrast to the president's traditional all-male press corps. This practice proved a great success. As Hick anticipated, they brought invitations from across America, to visit and talk to groups, and to give both press and radio interviews. Next Mrs. Roosevelt began her daily newspaper column. Soon this new sort of first lady was on the go from morning to night. While one could see her fatigue from this strenuous schedule, it was plain that my grandmother wouldn't have it any other way! The president approved and encouraged the emergence of his wife's new identity. It was, of course, a useful one, and a boon for him.

Lorena Hickok and Eleanor became close friends. My grandmother was very responsive to "Hick." (This is what we all, young and old, called her.) Their letters show an unusually close relationship. My grandmother needed the love that Hick offered, and at the same time, she recognized in Hick someone who very much needed her. Hick, with little money of her own and ill from diabetes, now moved into the White House, at Eleanor's behest. As Lash writes: "She had learned to compensate for her inability to let herself go by doing things for her friends."[1]

But my grandmother drew the line—as she always had—at physical intimacy. Hick, after having had an active lesbian partner, most likely wanted to pursue that course. As Eleanor's infatuation waned, she recognized Hick's continued yearning and loneliness. She even wrote to her urging her to get married and have a family. It is on the basis of their correspondence from the early days of their friendship that—to this day—Eleanor is still thought to have been sexually engaged with Hickok.

However, what I believe people ignore is that such passionate exchanges through letters was a time-honored form of women's communication—a vestige of centuries past and much practiced in the Victorian era, before Sigmund Freud made these chaste relationships too difficult to imagine. We forget, or have no conception of, how a wife used to be tied, legally and practically, to her husband. He was pretty much free to do what he wanted, but she was bound to church-derived discipline and the vows that marriage laws imposed. Hence writing letters to express their passions was one of the few avenues open to married women.

After Hick, it wasn't too long before my grandmother developed another close relationship (I guess we could even say, "fell in love again"). Joseph P. Lash was a young man who was obviously very bright, very sincere, and very devoted to Eleanor Roosevelt. And, like all his predecessors, he needed her, just as she, in turn, needed him. He was a staunch ideological socialist—typical of his time, a Brooklyn Jewish intellectual. Eleanor's letters to Joe were equally as passionate as the ones she had written to Lorena Hickok. Just as she had encouraged Hick to find someone to marry, so she urged Joe—pushed, I would say, from reading my grandmother's letters—into a courtship and marriage with Trude Pratt, a longtime friend of Eleanor's and another person who craved Eleanor's attentions just as much as Joe Lash did.

At the end of World War II, David Gurewitsch had become Eleanor Roosevelt's doctor in New York; he had been introduced to her by Trude Lash. A year later, when Gurewitsch needed to go to Switzerland to be cured of tuberculosis, air travel was nearly impossible to arrange so Eleanor, as a U.S. delegate to the United Nations, made him her "companion" in order to get him a plane reservation. Stranded for two days in Dublin by bad weather, Eleanor nursed David. They sat together and talked and talked, my grandmother reported. Perhaps during this quiet period their mutual understanding became obvious to both of them. Certainly, their companionship was plain to me when I met Dr. Gurewitsch in Paris the following year. My grandmother had found yet another person to whom she could dedicate her passion for unsullied love.

My impression of David was of a person who had all the attributes my grandmother would have liked to find in her own sons. Soft-spoken, thoughtful, courteous, occasionally mischievous, David had an effete quality, a sophistication, which I associated with well-mannered European men. Coming from Vienna, he spoke English with a cultured accent. My uncles felt his manner "foreign," insinuating that he might well be homosexual. To the contrary, as I later learned, the charming David avidly pursued the ladies of New York—a genuine man about town, rivaling anything my uncles might have achieved. But David was discreet, and my grandmother knew little, if anything, of that part of his life.

After his marriage to Edna Perkel in 1958, I noticed David's passion waning, although my grandmother's did not. According to Edna, Eleanor continued her passionate outpouring of love letters, and David remained my grandmother's particular friend as well as her medical physician until her death in 1962. In recognition of the fact that she had never once received a medical bill from him, my grandmother's will left to David and Edna the top half of the townhouse on East Seventy-fourth Street, which they had shared in New York City for many years. There is a plaque identifying their residence.

I have but scratched the surface in my brief sketches of the men and women with whom Eleanor Roosevelt engaged in her search for love. Much more could be written about each of these relationships. All of her intimate friends were interesting people. As I have noted, I have the advantage of having known them all, some quite well. But when I review them together I see no pattern, no particular similarity among them. Except for one thing: none of my grandmother's "crushes" were for people of her own social class. And what they had in common was that they all, in some way, needed her.

There was never anything clandestine about my grandmother's passionate friendships with both men and women. It is not by accident that I was acquainted with the lot of them; they were part of my extended family. They were often to be found at our dining table, either at Hyde Park or the White House. Within the family we may have gossiped about the latest arrival, but the remarks I heard, while often catty, were open and freely exchanged. My grandfather always welcomed warmly the latest of his wife's "flames."

So how did Eleanor Roosevelt—ever in the public eye—remain free of scandal? She did it by maintaining a chaste relationship with all these close friends. In fact, she took as gospel that lust was a sin, a descent into disaster—"down the slippery slope" was the phrase to which I was introduced as a child. My grandmother's particular fear of sex—indeed, fear of any physical closeness—was applied not only to herself but also to her children. All I ever received from her was a pat on the head indicating approval. If she had lived to hear of the description "touchy-feely" she would have shuddered. (As a child my mother's hands had been tied to the sides of her bed to make sure she "didn't touch herself.") However, toward the end of her life Eleanor seemed to find it easier to pick up babies and express her pleasure in holding them.

Drinking too much was the same story. All intemperate behavior, particularly when habitual, meant being out of control. Loss of control was something she feared, something she dreaded for herself as well as for others. And from observations of my grandmother's feelings, loss of control was potentially a loss of personal integrity. She wrote, "Anyone who does not have self-control to live within the bounds of moderation is a slave in the very truest sense of the word."[2] This could mean just the slurred voice after one too many cocktails or her brother, Hall, arriving uninvited for supper at the White House—dead drunk.

From conversations with my mother, I learned that both Eleanor Roosevelt and Sara Delano Roosevelt identified with those Victorian women who considered sharing the marital bed to be a duty, for procreation, nothing more. Blanche Cook, author of a three-volume biography of Eleanor, belittles this view, but Eleanor grew up with and retained throughout her life many restraints and inhibitions now considered old-fashioned. If you were around her it was very apparent. My grandmother emphasized to me, usually through stories, that personal and societal restraints were useful as behavioral guidelines. Without them one would "stray" and become "lost" (words right out of Sunday's lessons). From her father to her brother and then to her sons, she observed with sorrow where indulgence had led them in life.

Eleanor's religious background was very influential in

forming her keen sense of morality. The General Confession from the Book of Common Prayer, which she regularly used, begins thus:

> Almighty and most merciful Father; We have erred, and strayed from thy ways like lost sheep. We have followed too much the devices and desires of our own hearts. We have offended against thy holy laws. We have left undone those things which we ought to have done; And we have done those things which we ought not to have done; And there is no health in us.

Though she never talked much about God or the saints, it seems to me that my grandmother searched for a purity in life that was right out of the teachings of Jesus. She sought the ideal. In her daily life she relied heavily on her integrity to guide her, as well as her strongly rooted sense of duty. For example, whenever FDR went home to Hyde Park for the weekend, Eleanor always moved from Val-Kill back into her small bedroom next to that of her husband in the Big House. She said she felt it was her duty to do so.

So, Eleanor wanted nothing but to love and to be loved? Simple? Yes. In theory, that is, if not in practice. For my grandmother, what was most important—indeed an imperative for her—was the opportunity to apply her spiritual beliefs in her daily life. And she worked at it, often with a puritanical zeal. It was not uncommon to find my grandmother still at her desk dealing with correspondence at two o'clock in the morning. So many of those letters were from people who needed her!

One final anecdote should be shared, one that further illustrates the unrealistic idealism of my grandmother. Stepping aside from the sequence of Eleanor Roosevelt's personal series of romantic episodes I turn to my grandmother's promotion of the ideal marriage—that of my mother and John Boettiger, my stepfather. Eleanor set the pace, the ideal, and promoted it. She was behind it, I know, one hundred percent.

I was barely two years old when my mother separated

from my father, Curtis Dall. On FDR's campaign train in 1932 she met my future stepfather. He was a reporter for the *Chicago Tribune*, a major newspaper owned and run by the arch-conservative Col. Robert McCormick. It was said that they "fell in love" on the train and began to see each other even before we moved into the White House the following year.

From the very beginning, my mother and her own mother were closely entwined in the new romance, mine basking in her mother's support. Eleanor saw John as different. She approved of his not being from "society" (as all of her then daughters-in-law were), and being a newspaper reporter distanced him from Wall Street or other traditional professions. Eleanor Roosevelt was like a fairy godmother, even arranging that her cottage at Val-Kill be vacant so that "Anna and John" might have a private place for trysts. When my sister and I joined my mother in Washington, my mother's affair with John was already in full swing, openly accepted. (After FDR's election John was assigned to the *Chicago Tribune*'s Washington bureau.)

My grandmother had taken John Boettiger under her wing. She frequently invited him for supper at the White House. He became such a regular that the guards and ushers knew him well. He learned to ride horseback so that he could join my grandmother and mother, going with them to the White House stables at Fort Meyer. In effect my grandmother recognized John as her future son-in-law. She held her daughter and her fiancé to be very special, a couple whose love was to endure forever. All that was needed were arrangements for the divorces, for both my mother and for John.

My mother wanted to move quickly, but her younger brother Elliott jumped in with his own divorce plans and took priority. My grandfather suggested that two divorces in the family in the first year of his presidency was a bit much and asked my mother to delay hers, which she agreed to do. I feel that FDR also wanted to give his daughter another year before remarrying. But any sensible thoughts on my grandfather's part were more than mitigated by my grandmother's strong support for John Boettiger. John began writing to his future mother-in-law as "Dear LL," the LL standing for Lovely Lady. When my mother and stepfather wrote to each other, they referred to themselves as "US."

The special relationship Eleanor Roosevelt fostered for my mother and future stepfather was to be a love that was unique, indeed unlike other marriages. Continual devotion was to be the hallmark. My sister quickly sensed this exceptional romance and was fully supportive, indeed quite demonstrative. I remained less than responsive, counting flies on the wall whenever the mushy stuff got too much for me. But I quickly sensed that John was, in the minds of my mother and grandmother, to be an antidote to my being without a resident father. That my actual dad, very much banished to the sidelines, continued to be condemned with such open hostility was puzzling for me. Perhaps it was one reason why I never grew close to my stepfather.[3]

In 1934 my mother took Sis and me to Reno, Nevada, where six months' residency was required to obtain a divorce. My grandmother continued to entertain John regularly at the White House and wrote of trying to take care of him in my mother's absence. When my mother's divorce was completed we returned to the White House. But now it was John's divorce proceedings that held up the marriage. When the marriage finally took place a year later it proceeded in secretive fashion, which of course increased the press coverage. My new stepfather and my mother moved to New York City, leaving Sis and me at the White House. Soon afterward we moved to New York, too, and then across the country to Washington State where my stepfather had a new job. My grandmother was a frequent visitor to us in Seattle, even one year giving up Christmas with the rest of the family in the White House to be with us in our new abode.

The special relationship between my mother and my stepfather that Eleanor Roosevelt had fostered remained in full view, and could be rather overpowering. As I record in my earlier book: "We did join Mummy and Uncle J for their cocktail hour when they came home. It was like a sacred ritual. Mummy and Uncle J, sitting opposite each other on the couch, began by raising their Martini glasses to each other and mouthing silently (but visibly) 'I love you.' Sis and I would turn away and look at each other with resigned expressions of disgust." This vision of an extraordinary marriage—"Anna and John"—was to be maintained for some time to come.

As I read the correspondence of that era, particularly letters between my mother and her mother, I see my mother constantly seeking her own mother's approval. Even inaccuracies written about me were presented to gain this approbation. The same is true of my stepfather's letters to his mother-in-law. Eleanor Roosevelt was not just their fairy godmother but also their guide and mentor. They regularly turned to her for approval and affirmation.

At Christmastime in 1939 we returned to the White House. This visit showed me how fully engaged my grandmother was in supporting "the Boettigers." (I had been strongly pressed, and had reluctantly agreed, to start using the name Boettiger instead of my father's.) Although the White House would be full of family and guests for the holiday, my grandmother wanted, she said, to keep the Boettigers together as a family group. She was adamant that we were to occupy the entire west end of the living quarters for the president and his family.

Here I must explain: On the White House second floor there are four grand suites, one in each corner, each having a large gracious sitting room and bedroom with a small dressing room and an adjacent bathroom. My mother and John were in one of the large rooms and little Johnny, my new half-brother, in the dressing room close to them. My sister was placed in the comparable suite on the other side of the wide hallway, with me staying in the adjacent dressing room. Sis was occupying the room the Queen of England had once slept in. My mother and stepfather stayed in the one assigned to the king. Later Prime Minister Winston Churchill would have my sister's room. In other words, "the Boettigers" occupied the prime space.

That the Boettigers occupied the entire west end of the family's living quarters did not please my uncles and aunts at all. They saw their own children shoved into the third floor. But Grandmère was very firm and ignored the flak. Her explanation about "keeping the Boettiger family together" was one that brooked no dispute.

Behind all of this was her vision of a marriage where love would endure no matter what the obstacles were. Unfortunately, there were many. John Boettiger proved to be quite neurotic, not sure of himself, especially about his role as the president's son-in-law. My mother went through many hoops and loops just trying to maintain her husband in the mold set out by her mother. Psychologically supporting him turned out to be a full-time occupation for her.

This whole romantic dream fell apart after the war and was triggered by my mother and John's abortive effort to start a newspaper in Phoenix, Arizona. First my stepfather had an affair and then asked for a divorce. My mother was humiliated. Phoenix was a small town in those days, 1946–48, and she was the object of much nasty gossip. She also learned that John had been regularly undermining the financial viability of their joint enterprise. So, of course, he had to resign as publisher and then move out of our home. The ideal marriage was over.

My mother was indeed devastated. My grandmother, disillusioned. Still, she continued to support this favorite person whose letters to her always began "Dear LL." She attributed the demise of her dream for the two of them to a kind of mental breakdown, which John Boettiger's subsequent suicide seems to have confirmed.

In my view much of the sad conclusion of my mother's second marriage was in fact due to the romantic idealism of my grandmother and to the positioning of "the Boettigers" at a completely unrealistic level, one quite out of reach of normal human beings—hence doomed to failure. In something of the same way that my grandmother engaged in those close, loving friendships I have earlier recorded, she created a falsified model for a perfect matrimonial union. Of course they are responsible for having accepted it—hook, line, and sinker. My mother would have done nearly anything to gain her own mother's approval—or to avoid her disapproval. John Boettiger dearly had wanted acceptance into the inner circle surrounding the president, and to a degree that none of us really grasped. His identity was totally wrapped up with his recognition as FDR's son-in-law. But fostering and actively backing this wholly unrealistic vision of a marriage made in heaven was Eleanor Roosevelt.

I spent my younger years in the White House, but from age seven until age seventeen, when John left our home in Phoenix, I lived in the Boettiger household. As I look back upon those years I see my mother constantly needing to bolster John's ego. This was necessary because her husband seemingly was unable to sustain his interest (and his confidence) in any project. I later learned from my mother that John was already speaking about leaving his job as publisher of the *Seattle Post Intelligencer* when we had been but three to four years in Seattle. When he went into the army in 1943, John Boettiger left my mother with a four-year-old son and two teenagers, my Sis and me, both off at boarding schools. If we hadn't had our grandparents' home at the White House to move back to, I don't know how she would have coped. My grandmother's help was essential. Even after his later having that affair in Phoenix and then divorcing my mother, she would still invite John, at his request, to her home at Val-Kill to discuss his problems.

I record this not only to provide another illustration of my grandmother's idealistic faith in the possibility of a "perfect love" but to show how destructive such a belief can be when it is directed toward others. Eleanor Roosevelt was usually against excess of any kind, especially when she observed anyone exhibiting compulsive behavior. But her own passion to experience an unsullied relationship, or to foster such, was a shortcoming.

12

"Hick," My Grandmother's Close Friend

As I have written, Eleanor Roosevelt's infatuation with Lorena Hickok is well known, though whether Eleanor knew of her friend's long history of lesbian relationships is unknown. At least, this is what I believe.

The continuing relationship between the two women ended only with Eleanor's death. The passion had evaporated after the first few months, at least on Eleanor's part, but the friendship endured. Eleanor continued to see Hick regularly, although as the years went by, less and less. As time passed, it was about my grandmother's sense of loyalty. But Hick was persistent, and Eleanor always responded.

I've already spoken of the ways in which Hick helped her friend Eleanor achieve her expanded role as first lady. Hick was as close to a formal adviser as Eleanor ever had. In fact Hick became such an integral part of the first lady's life that she resigned from her job as a reporter for the Associated Press. She felt that she could no longer be an objective reporter, and rightly so.

She had also become Eleanor Roosevelt's closest friend. The letters they exchanged are the best indication of their intimate relation, but, as already noted, Hick had one view of their intimacy and Eleanor quite another. As with all her passions, my grandmother always wanted *to do something* for any object of her affection.

It became apparent that Hick was not well. Realizing this, my grandmother stepped in, first helping Hick to find occasional work and then most visibly inviting her to live in the White House. Hick occupied the small northeast corner room next to the large Lincoln bedroom just across from Eleanor's own suite. She joined us all for breakfast in the West Hall. She became part of our extended family and another of my second grandmothers.

Unlike Missy, my grandfather's secretary—who lived in a small suite on the third floor—formerly occupied by the White House housekeeper—or Tommy, my grandmother's secretary—Hick was kept more at arm's length. As my mother rather disapprovingly noted, Hick was the only one of my grandmother's new friends to call her Eleanor. Seen as a "hanger-on," she indeed she attached herself to Eleanor for the rest of my grandmother's life.

During the White House years, Eleanor continued to include Hick as much as she could, just never as much as I feel Hick would have liked. Hick's letters, now devoid of the more passionate expressions of her earlier correspondence, were always pressing my grandmother to spend more time with her. She continued to have occasional long stays in the White House and also to be financially dependent upon Eleanor. My grandmother, though, was able to wean her away gradually, helping her find a small house for herself on Long Island as well as a job with the New York State Women's Division of the Democratic Party. (Hick did have substantial experience in politics as a professional writer.) Eleanor had also arranged for Hick to work for Harry Hopkins, where she was assigned to take a long motor trip in order to report back public reaction to the Works Progress Administration projects under the direction of Hopkins. The accounts she sent in were very well received and still considered basic background for those researching the Great Depression.

Upon leaving the White House after her husband's death, Eleanor Roosevelt continued to see Lorena Hickok, despite the fact that her affections had long since been directed toward Joe Lash, and would soon change again to David Gurewitsch. But my grandmother is renowned for her unfailing loyalty to friends. She kept regularly in touch with Hick just as she regularly saw Esther Lape, one of the two people with whom Eleanor had begun her series of infatuations when she moved back to New York City from Washington in 1920.

Hick's continual pressure on Eleanor to see more of her was eventually annoying to my grandmother. She nevertheless responded. After Eleanor had made her place at Val-Kill her permanent home, Hick moved to nearby Rhinebeck into a small house (which I think Eleanor bought for her) about a half-hour's drive from Val-Kill. Periodically my grandmother would remember to invite her for supper and always included her for Thanksgiving and Christmas celebrations.

13

To Europe with My Grandmother

I had known for many years that my grandmother was a political pro. I observed this savvy in the White House and later with visitors in her New York City apartment on Washington Square. But it was at the United Nations in Paris in 1948 that I realized just how seasoned a professional she was. I listened while she discussed tactics with her advisers, and also with other UN delegates with whom she worked closely.

Because of her reputation in America as first lady and as "Mrs. Roosevelt"—a reputation that had crossed the Atlantic, being equally well known in Europe—she had an influence in UN circles no other American delegate had. As could be expected, this brought out annoyance among a few of the other U.S. delegates. But when it came to a tough assignment, particularly the need to confront the Soviet Union, it was to Eleanor Roosevelt they turned.

I was very proud of her having been chosen to answer Soviet Foreign Minister Andrei Gromyko in the General Assembly's debate on the contentious issue of the rights of refugees. None of the more senior American delegates wanted to take him on. Eleanor's straightforward speech—no mincing of words—was not the usual "diplomatic" approach. The delegates were delighted, full of praise for her. Even fellow delegate John Foster Dulles, a most prominent Republican, who came up to her later to acknowledge her effectiveness.[1] At a cocktail party afterward, Gromyko himself congratulated her.

My grandmother performing as the gracious hostess in Paris was hardly new to me. Her manner, warmth, and innate kindness had always been her hallmark.

But in Paris it was different. There she was truly focused, and I might even say, unusually calculating. Simultaneously hostess and political pro, she honed in on exactly what she wanted to accomplish.

Her goal was to get the United Nations' Universal Declaration of Human Rights (UDHR) passed at this session of the General Assembly.

At nearly every lunch and supper were three or four delegates talking intently, all under the influential presence of their hostess and chairwoman. I understood my own role—to keep the meal moving. For example, nodding to me to order more wine or start the cheese course, Eleanor would then return to the problems of the Indian delegate, Mrs. Hansa Mehta—accepting of the use of "man" or "mankind" in the UDHR draft text. Mrs. Mehta wasn't under instructions from her government to make this a contentious point; it was her personal crusade. She refused to recognize the use of "mankind" as covering both men and women.

My grandmother didn't disagree with such concerns, but instead felt the whole effort to pass the declaration might founder if Mrs. Mehta pressed too hard. Governments who were lukewarm about human rights in general, such as the Soviet Union, as well as so-called Catholic countries, would use the arguments raised by the Indian delegate to delay the whole process of work in the Third Committee. Hence, Eleanor would point out, the Universal Declaration on Human Rights would never reach the General Assembly for a vote. It would be delayed yet again, sent back to the drafting committee—and probably lost. Mrs. Mehta finally backed down.

Just as at the dining-room table in the White House, these meals, mostly at the Hôtel de Crillon, continued my education. But in Paris there was an additional advantage. In the morning, over breakfast, I often had a preview of the pending conversations at lunch or supper. Grandmère reviewed with me who the guests—her targets—were to be that day and what she wanted to accomplish. Because so much of the uneasiness over particular human rights articles in the draft declaration were related to religious and cultural norms, my breakfast briefings were an education about people in other parts of the world, what they cared about, their beliefs, or just habits long practiced.

For example, the American notion of the separation of church and state in our government was not, Eleanor said, accepted in most other countries, especially if there was a substantial majority of one religious group, as in what were seen as Muslim countries. That there were legitimate arguments on these questions really opened my eyes and made me aware of my own, typically American, self-righteousness. We, too, I now understood, were set in our ways, insulated by the thousands of miles of ocean on either side of our country.

My grandmother was candid, sometimes despairing, about how other of the American delegates—their ingrained attitudes blocking them—remained immune to appreciating cultural differences and understanding their political significance. There were members of the U.S. delegation who refused to acknowledge, or even consider, the validity of other views and how their own attitudes posed a serious obstacle in our working relations with the other UN delegations. Eleanor had repeatedly to point out that working in the United Nations' arena was a matter of continual negotiation, quite unlike the accustomed political landscape at home.

It wasn't that she had changed her values, she informed me, but that she had been forced to grasp how deeply other people felt about their interpretation of the same values. "I can't assume," she said, "that my interpretation, my sense of right and wrong, will be accepted by other people. I want to see things change in the practice of human rights as much as anyone else," she concluded, "but we will have to go slowly. And try to avoid being arrogant—a poor tactic if nothing else," she added with a knowing smile.

Now a seasoned delegate with much experience in the negotiating game, my grandmother would also point out how a people's attachment to their traditional cultural patterns was frequently exploited by politicians or government officials rigidly set against change. There was certainly nothing new about this, she reminded me—prejudice and fear-mongering among citizens has always been effectively used to block change. Setting down basic rights in a written document—a declaration that would, she hoped, guide governments—was hard work, uphill all the way. Additionally, we were now deep into the Cold War, a political reality that cast a shadow on nearly every item on the UN's agenda. And in the human rights area it was particularly touchy.

The role of the Roman Catholic Church was particularly vexing to my grandmother. The Vatican worked through the delegations of countries with large Catholic populations, nations where the separation of church and state was often still a theory in need of greater application. The Holy See's positions were, she noted, conservative, even reactionary, particularly on basic human rights related to women.

"I suppose I shouldn't be shocked," I would hear her muse. But considering the influence the church could bring to bear, if only with the Latin American countries, it proved a serious drag on obtaining the votes, and had been even during the drafting stage for a universal declaration. Due to continuous negotiations there was a danger of hobbling it with what my grandmother considered parochial views, mirroring the Vatican's authoritarian role. In passing, she noted that General Franco was still in power in Spain—and with the full cooperation of the church. Even in New York, she had found Cardinal Spellman's views very conservative on social affairs generally. A year later my grandmother would have a direct confrontation with him over the church's "growth in temporal power."[2]

With the Cold War in full stride, the Soviets' role was increasingly crass and expedient, tiresomely expressed but often effectively influencing the delegations of third-world countries. At every point, reported Eleanor, the Soviets wanted to water down or eliminate particular human rights, or put a twist on the meaning of some phrase that might embarrass Western countries, particularly the United States. With its very visible race problems—lynching, Jim Crow laws, cross burnings by the Ku Klux Klan, and job discrimination ("No Coloreds Need Apply" read the announcements)—we were easy targets, seemingly hypocritical when pushing for human rights. Eleanor Roosevelt, as the U.S. delegate, had a lot of explaining to do.

The Soviet government's seeming intention, Eleanor noted, was to see emerge from the United Nations a human rights declaration so innocuous and banal it could be ignored as useless, of no influence. To accomplish this aim they had now asked the General Assembly to review again every point in the draft declaration. They had already done this every step of the way—from the drafting committee to the Committee on Human Rights to the Economic and Social Council and now to the Third Committee. This made for an endless process bound to rekindle differences, a procedure that would lead to the General Assembly sending the document back to be studied and discussed again. Eleanor had taken the floor in the Third Committee to oppose the Soviets' motion, her voice quivering with rage and contempt. She won her point.

After two years of wrangling and hammering out the compromises that would constitute the declaration, its drafting committee had sent their agreed text to the Economic and Social Council. They, after reviewing it, passed it on to the

Third Committee, who, after themselves reviewing the most difficult parts of the draft again, finally agreed to recommend it to the UN General Assembly. This had been, thus, a process of review by no less than three bodies, on which the same representatives often sat.

At each stage and after provoking endless discussion, the USSR had agreed to the draft. Moving on in the laborious process, their delegates, however, acted as if they were ignorant of what they had already agreed to and now requested that every article be reviewed again. When they asked once more to do this, again in the General Assembly, Eleanor lost her normal "cool." She scolded the Soviet delegation as if they were recalcitrant children. The other delegates then not only voted the Soviets down, but were, many of them, amused and delighted at this display of Mrs. Roosevelt's anger. Undiplomatic it was, but certainly effective.

My grandmother hadn't been putting on an act. When she reviewed this with me over breakfast her voice was cold, with just an edge of harshness. She pronounced herself fed up with the Soviets' tactics of duplicity, particularly their playing on the prejudices built upon time-honored discriminations that were accepted practices in other parts of the world. They knew exactly what they were doing, she concluded. She was fed up with the Soviet Union's obstructionism. In the drafting committee and then later in the Economic and Social Council and finally in the Third Committee, she had worked for compromises, putting up with their negative attitudes. Finally she realized that it was a calculated effort on the part of the Soviets to destroy the Universal Declaration by not letting it be brought to a vote in the UN General Assembly. They would move to have it again reviewed, a slow process that could prevent the declaration from ever seeing the light of day.

Deeply disappointing to Eleanor (and to her advisers), indeed irritating, was the attitude of the State Department senior personnel such as Undersecretary of State Robert

Lovett. They would soft-pedal the importance of the declaration as being of little importance compared to the economic and political issues on the UN's agenda. The Soviets, seeing division in the ranks of the Americans, would take advantage of it, she realized.

It was touch and go if a UDHR were to be passed at this General Assembly. Some at the U.S. Mission were optimistic; others gave it no more than a fifty-fifty chance. My grandmother was in a state of anxiety. I had never before seen her so driven in her efforts. To obtain the vote, an overwhelming majority would be needed if the declaration were to be taken seriously by world governments. A close vote of approval would doom it to being ignored, she explained.

How much of this I was able to grasp—along with deciding whether I wanted honey or marmalade on my breakfast toast—I don't know. A lot of it stuck, mostly an appreciation of my grandmother's attitude, her passion coupled with her political savvy, and both blended with her will to achieve. Probably what made it a unique learning situation were the regular mealtime conversations, her own careful explanations, and the accompanying revelatory expressions of the faces of her dinner guests. Attitudes seemed to me to be much more important than "positions."

Whether at tea or over a meal, what was most remarkable to observe was just how little my grandmother paraded her knowledge and sensitive intuitions. She waited and allowed herself to be informed by those with a differing view. She then offered a complementary observation, perhaps thinking aloud—"I wonder if . . ." This would be followed by her floating the idea of a compromise that might accommodate opposing views—all the while serving a bit more chicken. Often observers might recognize what she was up to, but the most interesting reaction would be that of the delegate being asked to look critically at an ingrained social custom of his country. As ambassadors they might have the discretion to accept the suggestion, yet they needed to consider carefully the possibility of having their heads handed to them by their own government if they went too far. There was certainly good reason to be cautious.

She was not unmindful of how a delegate's government or foreign office might object to compromising the wording of an article, one that perhaps ran against their country's long-held traditions. She would even raise this point directly. It took guts for delegates to lobby their own foreign office for approval. But as the State Department advisers pointed out to me, we might yet have a declaration to present to the General Assembly and if we did, a huge credit was due to the gentle pushes from Mrs. Roosevelt. She made it happen.

With her guests, delegates from other countries, Eleanor Roosevelt often shared her own concerns and past experiences in the United States, frequently using discrimination problems as a reference point. It was telling. She was much more than an American emissary representing a position of the State Department. She was a citizen concerned for people everywhere, whose dedication to bettering conditions of life was well known. When she spoke, people listened. Her single-minded devotion to passing an effective Universal Declaration of Human Rights, and having it emerge from the 1948 session, was clearly recognized. Her exceptional integrity was unchallenged by all. Hence she played a unique role in the UN's complicated "circus." And she seemed quite at home with the divisive forces in play, far more so than other of the American delegates.

There were diplomatic professionals on the UN scene who weren't at all sure such a strong identity was proper for a delegate, an official government representative. Given the traditional approach of their kind, this assessment was to be expected. It seems inevitable that my grandmother's special influence within the UN caused disquiet within the State Department. However, without question, she always followed the instructions of her government, as was expected of all its representatives. And yet she was adept at lobbying the State Department to adopt her views. Also, she had access to President Truman that other U.S. delegates did not.

The other UN delegates usually knew when Mrs. Roosevelt was presenting a U.S. position with which she was uncomfortable. Still, their extraordinary respect for her integrity remained intact. Particularly with the representatives of smaller countries, Eleanor was both a delegate under instructions as well as an independent person with a keen sense of right and wrong, views that were not parochial. "Your grandmother listens and is open to our views," I was often told.

I didn't get to see the final act of this drama. The USS *America* left Le Havre for New York on December 10, and on board were most of the U.S. Mission staff, including Tommy and me. But later I had a firsthand report of the drama that took place in Paris in those last days.

After we had all returned home, just before Christmas, my grandmother had a conversation with Richard Winslow, the secretary general of the U.S. delegation to the UN and my cabinmate on the return voyage from Paris. As a result he kindly invited me to lunch the day before I departed New York to return home to Los Angeles.

At a restaurant near the UN, Dick regaled me with the firsthand report he'd received of the final vote that brought into being the Universal Declaration of Human Rights. The vote had been taken at the final session of the UN General Assembly, very late in the evening and early-morning hours. Dick certainly beamed as he watched the delegates rising to their feet after the final vote to honor Mrs. Roosevelt, recognizing how she had shepherded the declaration through the UN's subcommittees and committees for over two years. Such recognition had never before been accorded to an individual delegate, he told me. (And it would never be repeated, as far as I know.) Dick concluded his account by saying: "The kind of recognition received by your grandmother from the other delegates really shakes them up at State. It actually makes many of my colleagues uncomfortable." he owned.

Apparently the last session of the General Assembly was a fixture, traditions well in place, with everyone expecting the night to be long, the clock to be stopped at midnight and last-minute speeches varying from vacuous to vicious. Bickering had typically delayed a lot of the General Assembly's business, and so it did in 1948, right up to the last minute.[3]

Following correct protocol, the committees were taken in order for voting in the General Assembly, first the political, then the special political, and only then did the Third Committee's Economic and Social Council get a hearing. Its new chairman, Jacob Malik, a Lebanese Christian, "[then] one of the most respected figures in the General Assembly . . . [a] tall striking Arab," strode to the podium to place the Universal Declaration before the United Nation's membership.

Of Malik's address, Chile's Hernan Santa Cruz wrote: "He gave a detailed account of the whole long process of elaboration of the instrument that was being discussed. No one was able to do it with such authority, not only because of the responsibilities he had assumed in the process, but also by virtue of his lucid intelligence and his extraordinary talent for explanation."

Toward the end of his presentation, he emphasized that the declaration had the "common aspirations summed up so well in Franklin Roosevelt's Four Freedoms." He stressed that it "represented delivery on the promise of the UN Charter, which had mentioned human rights seven times but had not specified what they were or how they were to be protected."

Other speeches followed: the French delegate (René Cassin, who was to be awarded the Nobel Peace Prize in 1968) rebuking "the Soviets for their criticism of the Declaration as an incursion on national sovereignty." As reported by Mary Ann Glendon, in her book on Eleanor Roosevelt and the UDHR, the Chinese delegate, P. C. Chang, said the declaration was drafted in "a spirit of sincere tolerance of the different views and beliefs . . . [but] blamed 'uncompromising dogmatism' for accentuating disputes, saying there was at the present time 'a tendency to impose a standardized way of thinking and a single way of life.'"

The Soviet delegates looked on stonily expressionless. Then Foreign Minister Andrei Vyshinsky blasted back at the French, making "one last effort to have the matter put over to the next General Assembly on the grounds that the Declaration was still seriously defective."

Eleanor Roosevelt was in her seat, behind the sign reading "United States," the senior U.S. delegate left in Paris. Following the USSR, she rose to speak in favor of passing the declaration. Her words were measured, an obvious effort not to ruffle any of the feathers she had carefully arranged through various compromises. "It was not one of [her] best speeches," Santa Cruz records.

Rallying the Muslim states was Muhammad Zafrullah Kahn, representing Pakistan, at the time the member nation with the largest Muslim population. Again, according to Glendon, "he told the delegates that the article on religious freedom would have the full support of Pakistan." The struggles Eleanor had had with the Pakistan foreign office over the past two years were finally settled, and largely due to the influence of their ambassador. Kahn took great risks to state that "the freedom to change beliefs . . . was consistent with the Islamic religion."[4] Due to Kahn and Eleanor working together, I feel, all Muslim countries except Saudi Arabia voted yes on the declaration.

Then the delegates were polled. "The final tally was forty-eight in favor, eight abstentions, *and none opposed* [my italics]." The abstentions were the Soviet bloc plus the Saudis. It was a triumph, reported a jubilant Dick Winslow!

Although it is often quoted, pride makes me record again the tribute to my grandmother immediately made by the president of the General Assembly, Australia's H. V. Evatt: "It is particularly fitting that there should be present on this occasion the person who, with the assistance of many others, has played a leading role in the work, a person who has raised to greater heights even so great a name—Mrs. Roosevelt, the representative of the United States of America."

And then, by Glendon's report, "as the General Assembly rose to give her a standing ovation, a radiant smile illuminated her weary face." To my knowledge no one to this day has ever been so recognized in the United Nations' arena.

I believe that it was not just my grandmother being the driving force behind the UDHR—although I feel strongly that the people of the world would not have such a declaration if she had not been there to lead the effort. I observed enough of Eleanor Roosevelt working with the diverse delegates to know that she held a special place with them. Without question, everyone knew that while of course she represented the United States, her responses, her integrity, and her values represented an America that people believed in.

I have never been able to put my finger on the extraordinary influence my grandmother wielded within the UN sphere—nor has anyone else described it well. I saw it, as I closely watched her with the other delegates in 1948, but I could never explain it. After I went to work, myself, in the United Nations Secretariat in 1966, several delegates and staff members—old-timers—repeatedly told me of the unique role Mrs. Roosevelt had played at the UN. Their comments came from their personal experience; their impressions were always the same. There is no rational explanation for the phenomenon of "Mrs. R." One had had to see it to believe it.

Through the rest of that lunch, Richard Winslow and I went on trying to pin down Eleanor's unique influence within the United Nations. I'm sure we came up with the usual words of praise, the typical accolades my grandmother grew so tired of hearing when she was being introduced as a speaker— once humorously commenting to me that she felt they must be referring to someone else!

Before parting Dick asked me what it was like to be regularly in my grandmother's company. I blinked. I hadn't thought about that; I'd been in her company all of my life. It was an education, I said, or something like that. A rather limp reply.

When Eleanor resigned from her position as a U.S. delegate, at the end of 1952, Winslow wrote to her: "From top to bottom in the Mission you will stand as the finest symbol of all that is best in the United Nations and, in a personal way to each of us, as the finest type of civic leader, public servant, and working colleague."

14

Roosevelt as Commander in Chief

Under the Constitution of the United States, the president, among his many other duties, is commander in chief of the armed forces. Our Founding Fathers wanted civilian control over our generals and admirals. In wartime it becomes the primary occupation for the president. (The present situation is an anomaly—for many years now our American forces have been involved all over the world and yet we have not declared war, or at least not one sanctioned by the Senate, as the Constitution requires.)

In 1939, although only nine years old, I read all I could about the run-up to World War II, and redoubled my interest when the war formally began in September of 1939. The United States wouldn't be engaged until December 7, 1941, but the newspapers and magazines were full of Britain and France's declaration of war against Germany in response to the invasion of Poland. The following Christmas my family journeyed across the country from Washington State to Washington DC and the White House. There I heard much speculation about what Hitler might have up his sleeve— further invasions and conquests.

This period was already being referred to as "the phony war." Throughout that fall and winter of 1940 nothing warlike was yet happening. All was quiet on the western front—

Europe was waiting for Hitler to move. Then, in April, the German Panzer divisions struck quickly, subduing the Low Countries in a matter of days. Back in Seattle I had a hard time keeping up with the daily advances—Denmark, Holland, Belgium and Luxembourg—all now were occupied. Within a few weeks the headlines featured Dunkirk and the impending disaster of the British Expeditionary Force positioned there on the French coast. It was expected that the German army would simply push them into the English Channel. The extraordinary evacuation of the British troops from Dunkirk was riveting. Then France surrendered. The British were left alone to fight the Nazi regime. These events happened very quickly.

During this critical period my grandfather had made it plain to family and friends that what was happening across the Atlantic might soon become our war. He and my mother were frequently on the telephone, she getting the news from him just a bit ahead of the newspapers. From her I learned about the isolationists in Congress and the reluctance of most Americans to again engage in a war overseas, even though there was great sympathy for the British people.

An invasion of the United Kingdom was thought to be next on Hitler's list of conquests. With the British army having left all their equipment on the beaches of Dunkirk, Britain seemed an easy prize of war. To listen to Prime Minister Churchill's stirring speeches mobilizing his country's people was exciting for me. At the same time, my mother was reporting that my grandfather was deeply frustrated over being blocked from sending aid to Britain due to the Neutrality Acts passed by Congress.

His hands were tied. He saw Britain as America's first line of defense. It wasn't just the isolationists in Congress stopping him; it was obvious from the polls that the American public was in agreement. With an ocean on either side of us, we felt a false security.

Although a young boy during this prewar period, I was better informed than most of the adults that crossed my path. Recognizing my keen interest, my mother was good at passing on what she learned in her conversations with my grandfather. I began collecting more books about the navies engaged in the conflict. My grandfather had already given me three books that I pored over, including the 1940 edition of *Jane's Fighting Ships*.

By 1943 my stepfather was assigned overseas. He had thought—wrongly, as it turned out—that FDR would make him one of his military aides. Though FDR's four sons, my uncles, were in the armed forces, none were made presidential aides during the war, and neither was my stepfather. Instead, he was sidelined with an assignment to "military government."

Because of travel restrictions, my sister and I stayed on the West Coast until the summer of 1943. We then crossed the country to the White House to join our mother and little brother there. It was indeed a homecoming for me. I hadn't lived there since 1937.

Compared to my experience of living in the White House when I was a child, I found it a completely different place as a teenager in 1943. At the center of the changed atmosphere was my grandfather. He was now completely involved with his role as commander in chief of the armed forces. This was his priority and it occupied him totally. For example, I could not help but notice how my grandmother had a difficult time engaging him in domestic issues, in spite of her introducing them at the dinner table—the very same subjects that in previous years would have been at the center of FDR's attention.

He now spent longer hours in his office and often retreated after supper to his study on the White House second floor for further work, or perhaps for private meetings. His regular morning briefing with his personal staff was maintained, enabling him to keep abreast of a wide range of issues.

As Missy, FDR's longtime secretary, was soon unable to continue her duties due to a debilitating stroke, my mother stepped in to do some of the confidential chores that otherwise would have been handled by Missy. Not an official staff member, my mother worked—unpaid—in her spacious bed-sitting room, just down the hall from FDR's bedroom. Her desk was a card table with a pair of telephones on it. Whenever I was home from my boarding school I spent many hours sitting there, absorbed by the goings-on.

Regularly I read the newspapers and magazines delivered to her and, even more enlightening, I listened avidly to the dinner table conversations. Guests might be cabinet members, Supreme Court justices, or government officials. The key to the inclusion of some and the exclusion of others was their ability to be amusing and entertaining. Meals were FDR's time for relaxation.

My grandmother often encroached upon this leisure time of his by including her own guests at the dinner table. Once, when her close friends Sgt. Joe Lash and his wife, Trude, were there at supper, she announced, "Franklin, Joe has observations about his time in the Pacific War theater [he had just returned to the States], which I think you would find interesting." FDR immediately turned to Joe who, obviously uncomfortable, began to tell his story. We all listened attentively.

In those years I learned to keep my mouth shut about what I was hearing. I shared nothing with my schoolmates. For example, I knew well in advance about the date for D-Day, the Allied invasion of Normandy. How could I not enjoy being on the "inside," especially with military leaders arriving regularly to see their commander in chief?

To my great pleasure I was once asked by my grandfather to join him and Admiral Leahy, his chairman of the Joint Chiefs of Staff, at lunch. We ate from the edge of FDR's desk. Leahy had looked a bit startled as I came into the Oval Office to join them, but my grandfather reassured him by saying I was a great navy buff, and with a naval career in mind. I pulled my chair up to the desk and listened as the two men went on with their review of events, Leahy was rather stiff and colorless but straightforward, while FDR was serious and probing. I was not only "seen but not heard," I was probably not even seen. I focused on my chicken sandwich and a bit of salad. Dessert was ice cream—in my honor—my grandfather explained, as normally he skipped having it. At the end of the meal, my grandfather presented me a small ship model from among the many items on his desktop. It was the Brazilian battleship *Minas Gerais*, which I still have on my own desk some seventy years later.

Just before I returned to boarding school I again had an exclusive lunch with my grandfather, this time on the lawn beside the West Wing. His guest was his running mate in the 1944 presidential election, the senator from Missouri, Harry S. Truman. Again it was just the three of us. Over the usual chicken sandwiches, my grandfather reviewed the war's progress and particularly his problems with Winston Churchill over planning for the postwar era. Right after dessert my grandfather dismissed me saying he had a confidential matter to discuss with Senator Truman. My guess is that he informed his potential vice president about the Manhattan Project, in which the United States was developing the atomic bomb.

It wasn't until much later, when I read in more detail about FDR's role as commander in chief, that I came to understand just how purposefully my grandfather was focused on running the war. Even though he only intervened with his service chiefs when political implications were involved—or when they were at loggerheads—he nevertheless kept himself extremely well-informed. For example, late in 1943, dissatisfied with the summaries of the intelligence reports he regularly received, he demanded to begin seeing the complete data that came into the Army Signal Corps and from Navy Intelligence. In the evenings, after supper, I would observe him retreat to his study to review this daily pile of documents. He commented to my grandmother that "they"—Navy Intelligence and Army Signal Corps personnel—just didn't see the geopolitical implications of the information they were providing. The usual briefing papers one reads about being given daily to the president were not sufficient for FDR.

It was rare that my grandfather had appointments regarding the war outside of the Oval Office in the White House West Wing. It was there that he maintained his regular contact with Admiral Leahy, General Marshall, General Arnold, and Admiral King. Even before the Joint Chiefs were formed— before Pearl Harbor—it was in the Oval Office that he met with them.

There is a basic misunderstanding about the role of the White House Map Room, which was established to give the president a visual picture of the movement of troops and ships. But that was not where FDR conducted his role as commander in chief. I found that George Elsey's memoir, *An Unexplained Life* (originally published in 2005 and recently reissued) overstates the functions of the Map Room. Elsey had been a young naval intelligence officer during World War II. This view of it is reflected as well in the Roosevelt Library's recent exhibits at Hyde Park. As far as I'm concerned, it is all off the mark.

The reality is that the president would show off his Map Room to important guests like Winston Churchill, but it was never intended to duplicate the British prime minister's underground den (within walking distance of 10 Downing Street) from which he directed British forces around the world. No one seems to remember that Churchill was also minister of defense as well as prime minister; having attended Sandhurst he considered himself a military person. Meanwhile Roosevelt absorbed a lot during his eight years tenure as assistant secretary of the navy throughout World War I.

Fairly regularly after visiting Dr. McIntire's office to have his sinuses unblocked, FDR might briefly stop by the Map Room to have a look and chat with the officers on duty. (It was conveniently located right next to the doctor's office.) It was more of a social visit; FDR enjoyed seeing things visually but he was already acquainted with what the Map Room displayed. Unlike Churchill, FDR left the day-to-day running of the war to General Marshall and Admiral King.

An important function of the Map Room emerged when Roosevelt began his overseas rendezvous with Churchill, and later with Stalin—well known as the Big Three. There was a need for a single place for messages to be sent and received as the White House had previously relied on the Army's Signal Corps and Naval Intelligence for communications when the president was traveling. With the president now regularly abroad, the Map Room took over this role as the center forwarding his messages.

The White House corridors were a marvelous place to meet people, especially in wartime. Once, when walking down the second-floor hallway, I nodded hello to a U.S. Navy admiral, a full admiral. He was waiting outside FDR's study. Then I recognized who it was: Admiral William "Bull" Halsey! So I stopped, pulled up a chair, and we chatted. Of course I informed him that my goal was to attend Annapolis, the U.S. Naval Academy. Perhaps he was surprised at the amount I knew about the ships in his Pacific fleet. We talked amicably until a voice from inside my grandfather's study rang out, "Come in, Bill!"

But it was the conversation at the cocktail hour and at the dinner table that gave me a real sense of how FDR personally exercised his responsibilities as commander in chief. It was there that I learned, for example, how FDR left it to the British military leaders to inform Mr. Churchill that his idea of invading Crete was inadvisable, hence FDR could avoid confronting Churchill directly. Maintaining a working relationship with the British leader was not always easy but the president worked at it, and succeeded, often letting some of Churchill's outlandish ideas die of their own weight. FDR was always the politician.

After World War II, there were historians who judged Franklin Roosevelt as showing moderate involvement in his role as commander in chief, perhaps in comparison to the ever active Churchill. Roosevelt was criticized for leaving the running of the war mainly to the military leaders. But in the last twenty years this view has radically changed. Two recent books illustrate this: *No End Save Victory: How FDR Led the Nation into War* by David Kaiser and *The Mantle of Command: FDR at War, 1941–1942* by Nigel Hamilton. As one commentator on FDR, Alonzo L. Hamby, has written: he "displayed a grasp of grand strategy and tactical matters exceeding that of his military commanders."

An older work, but essential for understanding how FDR functioned, is by Eric Larrabee: *Commander in Chief, Franklin Delano Roosevelt, His Lieutenants and Their War*. He writes: "The President generated around himself an atmosphere of calm; his office was well organized and ran smoothly. What a contrast to Winston Churchill's where, as Harry Hopkins reported, the guns were continually blazing in his conversation." Larrabee continues describing FDR's leadership: "From this restraint and absence of bravado on the president's part comes much of the misapprehension that he refrained from involving himself in the war's direction. He marched to his own internal rhythms."[1] In my own words, my grandfather knew where he was coming from; he also knew where he was going.

His death in April of 1945, only a few weeks before the end of the war in Europe, blocks our seeing how clearly he had been mindful of the postwar world that would soon emerge, the advent of the Cold War.

There are good reasons for reviewing the approach of the American president and its contrast to that of British prime minister, who had to function in a fragile wartime coalition government. Churchill felt his War Office and Admiralty worked too slowly and were unimaginative. (Surely not as imaginative as *he* was!) Churchill considered himself an equal with his military chiefs. He had, after all, graduated from the Royal Military Academy at Sandhurst, the British equivalent of West Point, had served in the army, and had kept up with weaponry development since World War I. Then he had served as First Lord of the Admiralty. In the years prior to the British entering World War II, he was considered the Member of Parliament who knew the most about the armed forces.

FDR had been assistant secretary of the navy during the eight years of President Wilson's administration. He knew the navy well and once commented:

> The Treasury and the State Department put together are nothing as compared with the Navy. The admirals are really something to cope with—and I should know. To change anything in the Navy is like punching a feather bed. You punch it with your right and you punch it with your left until you are finally exhausted, and then you find the damn bed just as it was before you started punching.

Unlike Churchill, however, FDR had not kept up with military affairs after World War I. From 1921 until he was elected governor of New York State in 1928, his preoccupation was trying to recover from polio. But my grandfather always had a worldview, one I knew well, having grown up with him and it. I believe that over the years his stamp collection had taught him more geopolitics than any college course. His backing of U.S. participation in the League of Nations in 1920, not a popular view among his fellow Americans, showed his political orientation. And he was a major force in the establishment of the United Nations.

But more important was the difference in style and focus between the two Allied leaders. As minister of defense, a position he held in addition to being prime minister, Churchill intervened regularly with his military heads—read General Sir Alan Brooke's memoirs to see how they felt about this— and was often at odds with them on strategy. Roosevelt could observe Churchill's putting forward diverting strategies that might further British interests in a postwar world, but were not militarily sound. This he did because, along with his Foreign Office, Churchill was keen to reestablish the prewar British spheres of influence in the world.

Unlike Great Britain, the United States had no central intelligence service until the Office of Strategic Services (oss) was formed during the latter part of the war, and the Central Intelligence Agency (cia) subsequently established. An effort had been made at the end of World War I to maintain our intelligence service but the new Republican secretary of state, Henry Stimson, rejected this idea. He reportedly said, "Gentlemen don't read each other's mail!" With such history behind him, my grandfather had to move cautiously to organize an American governmental intelligence organization.

The lack of cooperation between the U.S. Army and the U.S. Navy was a real burden for FDR. The British had established joint chiefs for their army, navy and air force in the early 1920s, but it was not until 1942 that the Americans did the equivalent. Up until then, the hostility among the services was a continual problem. Nevertheless, Roosevelt chose not to interfere with the daily running of the war, leaving that to his newly minted Joint Chiefs of Staff. Admiral Leahy was its chairman but he wisely let the leadership directives issue mainly from General Marshall. During the war the British and American respective Joint Chiefs of Staff worked together, although this wasn't easy since the British had much more experience in functioning this way.

Another major difference between FDR and Churchill was Roosevelt's focus on the political problems in a war that was indeed global. FDR looked to the future, especially the postwar political and social consequences of World War II. For example, he saw the British Empire—and the French and Portuguese empires, too—as fading out in the postwar world, with Churchill holding instead quite firmly to his prewar colonial vision. For example, more than once during the war, Roosevelt strongly advised Churchill to promise India that it would be able to run its own affairs after the war, thereby gaining the support of the Indian people in the war effort. Churchill refused.

When Churchill referred to himself as being "Roosevelt's lieutenant" in 1943 he was, I think, not only referring to the fact that the United States was now the major supplier of the Allies' war materiel, but was also, I feel, recognizing the president's visionary leadership. But that didn't mean Churchill had changed his longstanding position of maintaining the British Empire. For him that was the raison d'être of the war.

Larrabee further notes, that Roosevelt's flexibility "should not be allowed to obscure that of constancy." He continues, "The means might vary, the ends did not. For a man who made so much of keeping his options open, to take advantage of opportunities as they arose, and to sabotage any other decision-making machinery than his own, President Roosevelt was almost rigidly consistent in his overall geopolitical strategies for waging war."[2]

Referring to Churchill, Roosevelt, General Marshal, and Field Marshal Brooke, British historian Andrew Roberts writes in his recent book, *Masters and Commanders: How Four Titans Won the War in the West, 1941–1945*: "Roosevelt was the ultimate arbiter between the competing strategies of Marshall, Churchill, and Brooke." And Roberts concludes, "The man who most influenced the course of the war was the one who openly acknowledged that he knew the least about grand strategy: Franklin Delano Roosevelt."

I have nothing to add to that!

15

Franklin Roosevelt and Winston Churchill

No, it's not revisionist history. It is a choice. Was it or wasn't it? Was it for real or not? Were Franklin Roosevelt and Winston Churchill really attracted to each other as friends? Or was it simply a grand performance by two old political pros? It is, after all, important to choose between the two views, for it changes dramatically the background to how we see the unfolding of the events of World War II.

Was the personal rapport between FDR and Churchill special, transcending the bond that one might expect from two government leaders allied against the juggernaut of Nazi Germany? Speaking of a "personal relationship" raises the question: Was there a genuine friendship between the two legendary leaders?

Most historians, especially from Britain, conclude that the relationship was perceived through the cosmetic strategies of public relations efforts, at the time exactly what was needed for these men's political roles. Such historians believe that FDR and Churchill were two heads of government who got along well together—most of the time—but really simply smiled for the photographers. The prolific British author Max Hastings has called it "a friendship of state." He dismisses Randolph Churchill recording his father telling him that he and Roosevelt had made "a deep and intimate contact of friendship" during the three days they spent together. (I assume Randolph's reference is to Churchill's first visit to the White House in December 1941.)

If this friendship did go beyond that of two heads of state, Churchill took pains to hide it lest it appear "inappropriate," even dangerous, to his cabinet colleagues in London. There were those who had already expressed the fear that Britain's interests would be compromised if Roosevelt turned on his legendary charm. FDR never referred to their relationship, but at the dinner table he might make light fun of Churchill's "Colonel Blimpish" colonial attitudes. Yet his affection for his co-leader in World War II was, I believe, plain to see.

I think the difference between these two views is quite important for our history. We need to assess the dynamics of this extraordinary friendship, beginning with "what happened"—especially the way it was viewed at the time, by which I mean those early days after America had been forced to enter the war following the Japanese attack at Pearl Harbor. Strategic objectives then had to be set in place for war against Germany and Japan. FDR was now a full-time commander in chief of all U.S. armed forces while Churchill was not only prime minster in a wartime coalition cabinet but Britain's minister of defense as well. The two leaders' roles were very different, and made even more so by the way each exercised his formal mandates.

Most writers hold the hardheaded, it seems to me, view that here were two seasoned political pros simply playing their assigned roles. I can see their reasons, but I feel they ignore a lot of plain facts as well as firsthand observations. They do not pay attention to the playfulness in the correspondence between FDR and Churchill, seeing it merely as stylistic banter, a useful front for the usual wary relationship between nations, even when wartime allies. These writers point also to the strongly divergent views between the two men toward the end of the war to hammer home their opinion.

Roy Jenkins's comment in his biography of Churchill is

typical: "It is more probable that the emotional link between Churchill and Roosevelt was never as close as is commonly thought. It was more a partnership of circumstance and convenience than a friendship of individuals, each of whom . . . was a star of a brightness which needed its own unimpeded orbit."[1]

So is a genuine friendship between FDR and Churchill just a romantic notion? Someone like Jenkins might reply, "You're not serious!—two hard-boiled politicians like Churchill and Roosevelt?" To which I would respond, "Yes indeed!"

I feel their actual mutual sympathy was obvious to most of the people around them. Was Churchill being cynical when he referred to himself as "a former naval person," knowing Roosevelt's love for the navy? No. Churchill had the same soft spot for the navy. It seems to me quite normal for Churchill, who was First Lord of the Admiralty when their correspondence first began, to seek ways of establishing rapport with the president of the United States. And from the very beginning of their long correspondence it was FDR who led the way in establishing the friendly style, creating the amiable atmosphere between the two.

When they first met in 1941 on their respective warships in Placentia Bay, Newfoundland, producing the Atlantic Charter, the two national leaders also demonstrated the value of their rapport. Their meeting was marked by an easy relationship, not the usual, more diplomatic reserve.

Historians who downplay the importance of the friendship have evidence on their side. Churchill seems to have thrown up a screen to obscure the genuineness of the personal friendship. For this, we have not only his own writing, we also have the reports of people close to him, such as John Colville, his private secretary. Quoting Churchill himself, Colville wrote that he had engaged in a "concerted and calculated" wooing of FDR, and that he was willing to throw over normal English reserve to "charm" Roosevelt and to gain the president's willingness to bring America into the war. Colville didn't understand, nor did Churchill perhaps, that it would be the U.S. Congress that would have to be "charmed" if the United States was to come into the war.

Upon returning to London, Churchill went out of his way to minimize his relationship with FDR. At the time when he spoke to Colville—using him because he knew Colville would spread the word—Churchill was wary of the diverse personalities in his War Cabinet. Key members were his supporters but others were more reserved, feeling that Churchill needed to be controlled. Even members of his own Conservative Party, as well as the Labour Party opposition—including Cabinet Deputy Prime Minister Clement Atlee—felt that their prime minister was prone to impulsivity.

Also, influential Foreign Office professionals were edgy about Churchill's relationship with FDR, fearful that it was too close, too personal, and, God forbid, it might interfere with the Foreign Office planning. (As indeed it did.) From their point of view, Churchill's rapport with Roosevelt was plainly inappropriate for a British prime minister.

My stressing the friendship between the two leaders doesn't diminish the fact that Churchill was not without a well-developed agenda when he came in December 1941, after Pearl Harbor, to visit the White House. To put it simply, the British needed American aid, both material and financial, in order to continue the war against Germany. Once France had been defeated in 1940 they were on their own. Indeed they fully expected an invasion across the English Channel— until Hitler changed his mind and invaded the Soviet Union instead. However, by early 1942 they could anticipate soon being broke—and this was because the U.S. Congress insisted on the British paying cash on the barrelhead for any arms bought from America. There were no loans or credit.

Especially after FDR's resounding reelection victory in November 1940, Churchill believed that the president had the executive power—as a prime minister would have had—to move past an isolationist Congress and send aid to Britain. He didn't grasp the fact that even though Roosevelt was 100 percent behind Britain, his hands were still tied by Congress. My guess is he assumed FDR was only stalling for domestic political reasons. So that when he came to the White House for that December visit, it was with a definite plan to put pressure on the president for money and materiel. He had no choice. Even with the United States and Britain becoming allies after the Pearl Harbor disaster, he knew that without aid, and soon, Britain couldn't carry on much longer.

We must add to this the fact that Churchill, as I have already said, lacked a real understanding of how differently the game of politics is played across the Atlantic. The difference between a parliamentary form of democracy and one in which the executive and the legislative branches are purposely made separate is very important. Churchill's writings indicate that, while he surely understood intellectually the difference in form and structure, he did not fully grasp the political implications. Therefore he did not see as clearly as he might have that, from 1939 on, FDR was taking enormous personal political risks on behalf of Great Britain.

Over and over again he expressed his expectation that FDR *would now* be able to bring America into the war. Roosevelt, however, made it plain, especially in the 1940 election, that the United States would not enter the war without first being attacked. I should add here that FDR's efforts, prior to Pearl Harbor, to provoke an attack in the Atlantic from German submarines had not proved fruitful despite the many risks taken. As an American politician running for office, he could not have said otherwise, but with every one of FDR's recent political victories—the Lend-Lease Act, for one, not to mention his third-term reelection—Churchill always felt that *now* FDR could, if he wanted to, pull America into the war. Apparently he simply refused to see that Congress would have turned the president down if he had asked for a declaration of war against Germany. The Japanese attack on Pearl Harbor made all the difference. And even then it was only the precipitous action of Hitler unilaterally declaring war on

America that immediately brought the United States into the war against Germany.

The comparison between the political systems of the two English-speaking countries appears easy to grasp, but it isn't so. My course on the British political system at Columbia University when I did graduate work there was excellent, but when I moved to England I found that I really understood very little about the politics of the British parliamentary system, the way it actually works. And thirty years as a member of the Reform Club in London has amply illustrated for me how little my friends there understand the U.S. democratic system, our politics. After years of trying to explain and illustrate this to them, my conclusion is that making comparisons is only confusing and, often worse, misleading. So when I refer to Churchill's "lack of understanding," it is not meant as a criticism of his intellectual powers, it is just an observation on the complexity of trying to understand the American system from his point of view.

But back to that memorable meeting in Washington when the prime minister of Britain spent two weeks living comfortably in the White House. It was on this occasion that the friendship of FDR and Churchill was cemented. Correspondence and the brief Atlantic Charter meeting had shaped it, but seeing each other daily with time for banter and informal exchanges, especially when the two men were on their own, was very different. Indeed it was unprecedented and most unusual for a British prime minister and an American president to become chums.

What Roy Jenkins and others ignore, or feel to be irrelevant, is that Churchill and Roosevelt shared many cultural and class values. True, they did not have exactly the same background, but both been born into households of nannies and servants. And both went to schools proper to their status (though neither did terribly well). Each went into politics as soon as the opportunity arose, and succeeded.

Once in the political arena they were thought of as rebels,

upstarts, too big for their britches. Yet they both were recognized as competent and were appointed to senior government administrative posts while still young.[2] Still, the superiors of Roosevelt and Churchill kept a close eye on them, trying to rein in their enthusiasm in the exercise of power.

The British historian Robert Rhodes James has written about Churchill as "a study in failure." His career was indeed marked by serious ups and downs, being in and then being out—banished into the political wilderness—but his accomplishments while holding ministerial positions were recognized.

FDR's political career followed the trajectory of his cousin, and idol, Theodore Roosevelt. It was a star that rose and then suddenly plummeted. Like Churchill, he went into "the political wilderness" after eight years as assistant secretary of the navy. This was, of course, not because of any action of his own but for reasons of having fallen victim to the debilitating polio that left him crippled from the hips down, unable to get around without assistance. After having been on the national scene as vice-presidential candidate for the Democrats in 1920 and recognized as a rising star, he was quickly a political has-been. Thus, when Winston Churchill arrived at the White House in December 1941, he and his presidential host both knew well the victories and the defeats that mark all practicing politicians.

When he arrived for his stay at the White House, Churchill brought with him a small version of his Map Room. This was installed in the Monroe room of the White House, just across the hall from his bedroom, the same bedroom that Queen Elizabeth had used when she and King George visited the Executive Mansion. It should be noted that he pronounced himself immediately at home. He didn't have to adjust his habits to fit into the Roosevelt household. And it was the same at the family home at Hyde Park. My guess is that he was much more at his ease than he might have been if he'd been snagged into spending a couple of weeks at Buckingham Palace with the king and queen as his hosts.

There was a relaxed informality, owing much to my grandmother, which blended in with the accustomed White House formalities, a style Churchill would have found compatible. As his youngest daughter, Mary Soames, said to me, "We felt quite at home at your family's place at Hyde Park." We know from his aides that he also felt the same way about the White House.

Winston Churchill undoubtedly knew that the White House was the Executive Mansion of the president of the United States, FDR being chief of state as well as head of government. Hence the White House was something of a hybrid—a cross between Buckingham Palace and 10 Downing Street. But the prime minister was not in the least fazed by protocol ranking him one step down from his host, who was head of state, just as the king was in Britain. This is why it was FDR who always chaired the meetings of the Big Three wherever they met.

In the evenings after supper, they smoked and drank, and bantered. Serious business was reviewed but it was mixed with storytelling and, most importantly, a sharing of speculations and "what ifs." Both men liked to display their knowledge of the world beyond their own countries and the politics of the "spheres of influence" across the globe. It was a longstanding way of keeping the peace that had been the cornerstone of international relations since the Congress of Vienna, after Napoleon's defeat in 1815.

In the White House my grandmother took the prime minister's visit in her stride, but she was much concerned about their guest's proclivity for "staying up all hours, talking with 'Pa'—until two in the morning!" she said. For, as she noted, her husband was used to going to bed well before midnight. She said, "He drank whiskey right along with Mr. Churchill," and then added, "although not as much." The prime minister would have a nap in the afternoon, she reported, "while Franklin was at his desk" catching up on his work. "Yet 'Pa' didn't seem tired; indeed, he seemed to thrive on it." My grandmother noted that Mr. Churchill had members of the White House staff flabbergasted; they'd never seen imbibing on that scale. "He consumed an astonishing amount throughout the day," she said, then adding, genuinely puzzled, "He doesn't seem to show any effect from it!"

Quite aside from the alcohol, my grandmother reported that "Pa" and the prime minister seemed "to charm each other" and that she hadn't seen "father" so relaxed in another person's company for a long while. For me that is the key as to "what happened," the telling observation, indicative that the warm feelings between the two men were genuine.

One of the most revealing expressions of Roosevelt and Churchill's unusual relationship occurred at the regularly scheduled White House press conference. This fell on the first full day of Churchill's visit, in the late afternoon. FDR had invited the prime minister to join him. The two heads of state sat behind Roosevelt's large desk. The *Washington Star* described the scene: "Two great statesmen/showmen, sharing the star parts in a world drama that will be read and studied for centuries to come, played a sparkling and unique scene at the White House yesterday."

The Oval Office was crowded with reporters. Roosevelt asked Churchill to stand on his chair so the press could see him better. The British leader obliged and proceeded to shoot back answers to the reporters' questions, all the while waving his cigar to emphasize points. Alistair Cooke, then a young Englishman reporting from the United States for the *Manchester Guardian*, described it as "terribly exciting" and wrote, "Accustomed to commanding this room and this audience, Roosevelt sat back and delightedly—even proudly—watched Churchill cast his spell."

What I find amazing is one flamboyant politician inviting an equally flamboyant one to take over his stage and make it his own—which Churchill did. As *Newsweek* reported, "The smiling president looked like an old trouper who, on turning impresario, had produced a smash hit. . . . Some thought they detected in his face admiration for a man who had at least equaled him in the part in which he himself was a star."

This certainly doesn't square with the narrow view of Lord Moran, Churchill's physician. Not known for political sagacity, he pronounced that really all the two leaders had in common was the war. While more accepted authorities, such as the British historian David Adams, take a centrist view, describing Roosevelt and Churchill as having "a marriage of convenience," for me, that fails to take into account the importance of the trust a personal friendship generates.

Some historians might propose that the friendship between Churchill and Roosevelt was not dissimilar to the smile, winks, and nods we could observe between Ronald Reagan and Margaret Thatcher. Or, more cynically, was it primarily for the press, as when the Blairs and Clintons were photographed dancing together after supper in the White House State Dining Room? Neither of these images passes muster; the relationships were completely different—consider the time and circumstances. The word used by the press is one I don't like, "bonding." It covers everything from casual interaction to merely an expedient expression of compatibility and affection—as well as describing the real thing.

At the opposite extreme were those observers who gushed about the personal relationship—and that isn't helpful, either. In his recent book, historian Jean Edward Smith has a more measured approach, drawing from remarks by FDR's press secretary. Bill Hassett reported that Churchill, during his 1941 White House visit, made himself at home, walking barefoot, going wherever he chose whenever he chose. FDR enjoyed the same informality. And Smith quotes Lord Ismay, "There was something intimate in their friendship. They used to stroll in and out of each other's rooms." (FDR would of course always be in his wheelchair.)

A more dramatic report emerges from Alexander Cadogan's diaries (September 4, 1943—Washington DC—on a subsequent visit of Churchill to the White House): "He [Churchill] talks with the president till 2:00 a.m. and consequently spends a large part of the day hurling himself violently in and out of bed, bathing at unsuitable moments, and rushing up and down the corridors in his dressing gown."[3] Obviously Cadogan disapproved, a fitting response from a senior civil servant in the British Foreign Office.

But note Hassett and Ismay's details: FDR, crippled from the hips down, never strolled anywhere. And Churchill's padding about the family's quarters barefoot? Even I didn't do that! But the impression of "something intimate" is accurate. Early on in his first visit to the White House Churchill put on his "siren suit"—a one-piece coverall zipped from the crotch to the neck. Everyone else wore the usual tie and jacket.

In the morning, before Roosevelt went to the Oval Office, Churchill might walk down the long hall in his bathrobe to exchange a few words with FDR, who might still be having his breakfast in bed, or sitting in his wheelchair shaving in front of his bathroom mirror, and while that is a useful detail, what does it signify if it does not put their relationship into the context of intimacy?

But the Hassett and Ismay remarks are useful details to illustrate a personal relationship between Roosevelt and Churchill that was far more than the accepted gestures of friendliness between two heads of government.

Incidentally, Churchill did not enjoy Roosevelt's gin martinis and quickly reverted to his usual whiskey. I have described the scene in which once, at Hyde Park, being entertained at Cousin Laura Delano's home, Churchill was given one of her (in)famous rum cocktails. He took one sip and promptly dumped it on the stone floor of the terrace where they were sitting.

What I perhaps most fondly recall is my grandmother describing the two men sitting in the Map Room discussing the movements of their navies around the world as resembling "two little boys enjoying themselves in the bathtub with their toy boats." In this remark she was accurately recording the atmosphere, the informal and jocular working style of two men who, while occupying their respective positions of great power as president and prime minister, were still enjoying themselves. Gossip travels fast in the White House. By the cocktail hour, my grandmother had conveyed her amused observations of the two great men to my mother, who then passed the above story to my sister and me. We all giggled.

Everyone agrees that the relationship between these two legendary figures of the twentieth century, the prime minister of Great Britain and the president of the United States, our leaders during World War II, was extraordinary. But the question remains for historians—how genuinely personal was it? Was it just a show of collegiality between two political leaders sharing the responsibilities of wartime? Or was it, as I suggest, a personal friendship, historically quite unique among political leaders.

What I know about Churchill is all secondhand. What I know about Roosevelt is firsthand. I know my grandfather longed for the kind of rapport—both socially and at work—that he and Churchill were capable of generating when together. It came naturally to both men. They did indeed closely bond. They each had a "first-class temperament."[4] Of course their style of working together inevitably influenced their two countries' conduct of the war.

But my speculations upon the quality of the relationship between President Roosevelt of the United States and Britain's prime minister are impossible to verify. So let me speculate further, but in a different way. What if Lord Halifax had been selected to succeed Prime Minister Chamberlain in 1940? And, in fact, this very nearly happened. Robert Blake's short chapter, "How Winston Churchill Became Prime Minister," in his book on Churchill written with William Roger Louis, tells the dramatic story.

At that time, 1940, when Chamberlain's government clearly had to resign, Churchill had but a small band of loyal followers in Parliament, and even some of these mentioned Anthony

Eden as the better alternative. The majority of parliament's Conservatives plainly preferred Lord Halifax (Chamberlain's foreign secretary) as leader of the next wartime coalition. The Labour opposition had said it would serve in a coalition government under either Halifax or Churchill, but quietly let it be known that it preferred Halifax. So did Chamberlain, and so did King George.

The only person who didn't prefer Halifax—was Lord Halifax. That he was in the House of Lords and would have to lead the government from that position was a problem. Chamberlain proposed that it was not an insurmountable problem in wartime. But Halifax responded by saying that the thought of being prime minister in wartime gave him "a pain in the stomach." So it was Halifax, when meeting with Chamberlain and Churchill to settle the matter, who gave Churchill the nudge. That settled it. The king was "advised" to ask Churchill to form the next government. My guess is that Lord Halifax foresaw that he would have to give the crucial Ministry of Defense portfolio to the dynamic and articulate Churchill, who would then, and to a great degree, have represented the wartime coalition government in the Commons. This would have been intolerable for any prime minister—something that Chamberlain apparently didn't take into consideration.

What would the political dynamics have been like if Halifax had ignored the pain in his stomach and accepted Chamberlain's nudge? Lord Halifax would have been the prime minister of the next British government, a wartime coalition. If so, he might well have begun in 1940 to communicate regularly with the president of the United States. Probably he would have done so through the British embassy in Washington. But even if Halifax had written directly to FDR, as Churchill did, would his rather "Foreign Office style" have stimulated and amused Roosevelt in the way Churchill's letters did? Note the personal rapport that Churchill and FDR's letters indicated well before they met as prime minister and president at Placentia Bay, in the summer of 1941. This would not be likely to have been the case between Roosevelt and Halifax.[5]

Consider this. After the Pearl Harbor attack in December 1941 brought America into the war, would Halifax as prime minister have quickly gone to Washington to strengthen and develop Britain's relationship with President Roosevelt now that they were formally allies? Would he have stayed at the White House, except perhaps for a brief courtesy visit? Would he have sat up half the night gossiping and exchanging stories with his host? Would Halifax have even considered it appropriate for a genuine friendship to develop between himself and Roosevelt? My guess is: not likely! Probably he was one of those who disapproved, in principle, of Prime Minister Churchill's chummy rapport with America's president.

After Churchill became prime minister in 1940 he responded to FDR's congratulatory letter by noting, tongue in cheek, his new address—and then, in the same letter, he asked bluntly for a long list of materiel, from guns to destroyers. At the end of his letter, practically as a postscript, Churchill threw in, "I am looking to you to keep that Japanese dog quiet in the Pacific." Does that sound like an official exchange between two heads of government? Not at all! It was correspondence between two people who had already developed a confidence that enabled them to communicate with familiarity and humor. Such a style would have been, I believe, definitely "foreign" to a former foreign secretary!

Yet Halifax and Roosevelt, of course, would have made a point of getting along. A cordial working relationship would have, I expect, prevailed. Joseph Lash's subtitle for his book on Roosevelt and Churchill is *The Partnership That Saved the West*. Yes, true enough. But might it not have been accomplished just as well with Lord Halifax in tandem with President Roosevelt? Well, who knows? As Roosevelt would tell the White House press corps, "No 'iffy' questions, please!"

The subtitle of Lash's book makes a point. As far as conducting the war was concerned, FDR and Churchill did extraordinarily well. The dimension added by their very real friendship was more than a bonus; it sharpened and ignited both men. Their shared temperament was critical for directing major wartime decisions.

Still, the personal relationship between FDR and Churchill came under considerable strain as the war moved into its final stages. Inevitably, I suppose, differences arose between the two leaders, particularly concerning their views on the future of the British Empire and colonialism. Reviewing the Teheran and Yalta Conferences reveals this crucial disagreement becoming ever more prominent as postwar planning was discussed. During the war Churchill pushed for strategies that supported restabilizing the traditional British "spheres of influence" and had to be countered by FDR.[6] His military strategies were often aimed at this diplomatic objective. Luckily for the president, the British General Staff often agreed with the American military commanders on wartime strategies and joined him on overriding Churchill.

Winston Churchill's primary objective had always been to restore the British Empire to its prewar state. Stalin knew this, yet also assumed—not incorrectly—that the British Foreign Office would resume its prewar focus on anticommunism when the war ended. And so it was—with the new American president, Harry Truman, in agreement.

By the time of FDR and Churchill's meeting in Cairo, in November of 1943, the issue had to be opened. Cadogan's diary records it: "The prime minister has had to endure much with a good grace, including explanations from the president of other powers' 'higher morality.'" He quoted FDR: "Winston, you have four hundred years of acquisitive instinct in your blood and you just don't understand how a country might not want to acquire land somewhere else if they can get it. A new period has opened in world history and you will have to adjust yourself to it."[7]

The last sentence was Roosevelt's point—and was also for

Stalin's ears—but neither Churchill nor his successor nor the Foreign Office ever willingly took it in, as the postwar United Nations debates clearly showed. Also, I see Cadogan as obviously offended by the candor with which the American president had addressed his prime minister. Myself, I view FDR's bluntness as another expression of his personal relationship with Churchill.

At a very basic level, right from the gut, Roosevelt felt colonialism would be dead in a postwar world, particularly in places like India, the so-called jewel in the crown of the British Empire. FDR had not been shy about demonstrating his own view of colonialism; he sent two missions to India during the war, both unwelcomed by the British.

Also, he felt the French, for example, had ruthlessly exploited Indochina in the prewar period. See FDR's letter of January 24, 1944, in which he wrote to his own secretary of state, Cordell Hull, a concise memo stating in extraordinarily clear terms his position on postwar Indochina. Roosevelt felt that Indochina should come under trusteeship within the new United Nations Trusteeship Council. Churchill didn't voice an opinion but undoubtedly felt that both France and Portugal should have their colonies back, just as he insisted for Britain.

Churchill continued to be adamant that "not one inch" of the British Empire would be placed elsewhere. Trusteeship was FDR's baby. Unfortunately, toward the war's end Roosevelt had to retreat on this issue due to ill health, and his death ruled out his vision becoming the reality he had hoped for, a strong United Nations able to enforce its decisions. The sad fact is that none of the major Foreign Offices—American, British, or French—were eager to see a strong Security Council created. Britain's foreign secretary, Anthony Eden, was behind the unsuccessful push to make the defeated France a full member of the UN Security Council as well as becoming the fourth partner in the occupying forces of a defeated Germany.

FDR knew that keeping the peace needed to be addressed effectively in the postwar era. This meant creating a stronger and more effective organization than the League of Nations had been. The wartime allies, in fact, were already referred to as "the United Nations." FDR felt that including the Soviet Union in the project was essential if it was to succeed. Some senior people in both the State Department and the British Foreign Office had reservations about this, but Churchill felt compelled to agree with FDR.

However—and this is practically a contradiction of his agreeing with FDR—Churchill wanted the emphasis of a world organization to be at the regional level. FDR wanted a truly international organization with a strong Security Council, one dominated by the major powers. He thought it totally unrealistic to have the USSR sitting outside. And it was FDR, almost single-handedly, who obtained Stalin's agreement at Yalta.

Toward the end, however, there was one unfortunate incident that marred the two men's personal relationship: In his effort to win over Stalin and persuade him to support the Soviet Union becoming a member of the new United Nations organization, FDR exploited Churchill's well-known feelings about the preservation of "the empire" and his own opposite view. Churchill was deeply hurt, wounded even, to find his friend using him to make points with Stalin on a personal level, even if it was in a jocular fashion.[8] It saddens me to know that FDR died before he could make amends to Churchill for this expediency.

Although it was but a few months before the war ended when Truman and Atlee assumed the leadership of their respective governments, did we not all miss the flamboyant style of FDR and Churchill? Both the British and American people thought it natural for Roosevelt and Churchill to work well together, and to work as friends. For us they were not just our heads of government, they were leaders we can never forget.

After her husband's death, Eleanor Roosevelt wrote, "Besides the respect he [Churchill] had for my husband, which made it possible for them to work together even when they differed, he also had a real affection for him as a human being, just as my husband had for him." She concluded that it was a "fortunate friendship."

But the sentiment that I think says the most is one my grandfather wrote to Churchill: "It is fun to be in the same decade with you."

16

The Effect of FDR's Death on the Roosevelt Family

When Franklin D. Roosevelt died, what happened to my uncles, the president's well-known sons, his daughter, my mother, and my stepfather, the president's son-in-law? What happened to my grandmother? What happened to me? What happened to "Sistie and Buzzie"?

These are all questions I'd like to address. I can only report what I observed, or from conversations within the family. Occasionally outsiders would comment, with some of the most critical remarks coming from them—although some of the letters between my grandmother and mother were equally critical of my uncles, her brothers.

There can be no generalities except to describe the problem we all faced. The sun in our lives disappeared over the horizon. There was an afterglow for a while, but even that didn't radiate the easy recognition we had taken for granted when FDR was president. My uncles were used to being instantly recognized as the president's sons and my mother continued to be very conscious of how she behaved as the president's daughter. My grandmother was "Mrs. Roosevelt," and that was it!

My mother and stepfather's saga will be told in detail in chapter 17 because my sister and I were interwoven into that unfolding.

What happened to my grandmother can be put into one sentence. Having made her own reputation and renown in the White House, she simply agreed to President Truman's request that she represent the United States at the United Nations and extended her reach farther onto the world stage. It was like a second successful book built upon a previous best seller.

But what happens when the family's most famous person dies and one is no longer automatically in their reflected light? I have described it in my book *Too Close to the Sun*. It is the meaning of the book's title but not well understood.

So I begin with my uncles—what happened to them—because the forces they were exposed to, and their responses, were similar to mine. But being of an older generation, their stories, the conflicts created for them by their father's death, are more vivid, more illuminating, than my own.

There were certainly supporters standing by to hop aboard what they perceived would be the political bandwagons for both James Roosevelt and Franklin D. Roosevelt Jr. In contrast, Elliott had less personal attention but he did gain from the reflected recognition of joining with my grandmother in her Val-Kill enterprise at Hyde Park. John was left pretty much on his own, having made it plain that he had no public service ambitions. He was "in retailing," he insisted, not politics.

Quietly a group of informal advisers clustered around both James and Franklin Jr. Their purpose was plain; to devise the best path, which is to say, the quickest, to take their man into the White House as the successor to FDR—along with them, too, of course.

They were young, engaging, intelligent, and had outgoing personalities. And just as FDR had enjoyed being president, James, Elliott, Franklin, and John had equally enjoyed the limelight of being his sons. To a great extent that's who they were—FDR's sons. For James and Franklin Jr. this looked to be a good launching pad for their future national political careers.

Uncle Jimmy was the first to move in that direction, becoming elected to Congress from California in 1954. Earlier, in 1946, he had served as chair of the California State Democratic Central Committee, and in 1950 he had run for the governorship of the state but lost. The twenty-sixth district, however, was a safely Democratic one and he served not quite six full terms.

Uncle Franklin followed suit shortly afterward. I thus had two uncles in the House of Representatives. James had a good reputation for working hard and not throwing his weight around. Franklin's reputation focused on his excessive absenteeism. (I was told that the Speaker of the House, Sam Rayburn, was not impressed with either of them.)

My uncle Franklin, for his part, had entered electoral politics in 1949, winning a New York seat in the U.S. House of Representatives in a special election. He ran then as a member of the Liberal Party of New York. He then kept his seat—but as a Democrat—through three more elections. In 1960, he campaigned strongly for John F. Kennedy's nomination, and when Kennedy was elected president, he appointed Franklin as undersecretary of commerce. Afterward, leaving Washington, my uncle retired to manage his farm located not far from Hyde Park.

Uncle Elliott, as I said, had chosen to join my grandmother in reestablishing an estate at Hyde Park. She had been left some modest acreage surrounding her Val-Kill home in her husband's will, but she chose to buy back from the estate many more acres so that Elliott would have a real occupation managing its many activities—from farming to bees to tree planting. He lived at FDR's Top Cottage. For him, such a life proved difficult as he then had a wife on the Broadway stage. When he remarried, it turned out his new wife didn't like living at Hyde Park and so Elliott moved to Colorado to manage her ranch. Later he moved to Florida with another new wife, becoming mayor of Palm Beach for a short period.

Uncle Johnnie prospered in his chosen "retailing," working for several big department stores, and finally ended up a partner in the securities firm Bache & Company, where he oversaw the accounts of several important trade unions. Early on he had announced publicly that he was a Republican, and had given a seconding speech in support of Dwight D. Eisenhower's nomination for president at the Republican National Convention.

Though I don't think they fought very strongly against it, if at all, the primary identification of each of these four men, my uncles, derived from their earlier years, in the 1930s and 1940s, as the sons of my grandparents.

And what most impressed me about them was their self-assurance. I was in awe. In contrast I couldn't open my mouth without tremendous self-consciousness. With other people, I was always concerned about what they would think of me, what impression I would make. My uncles seemed unconcerned, as if they took for granted their acceptance and the special recognition accorded them. That had been their experience when their father was president, and it seemed, as far as their own attitudes went, to continue without a pause after his death.

What happened to my mother and stepfather after the sun went down for good is a different story. So is my sister's— and mine, too.

But let me return for a moment to my grandmother's "best seller" status and look at it more closely. Several months after Eleanor had been widowed, she received a telephone call from President Truman asking her to become one of the top five American delegates to the United Nations. Demurring, she told him she wasn't qualified. Truman insisted, and she finally agreed, and before long was off to London for one of the first UN General Assembly meetings. Assigned to represent the United States on the Third Committee, the Economic and Social body, the competence she demonstrated was quickly recognized. When her committee agreed to establish a subcommittee to draft a Universal Declaration of Human Rights,

Eleanor was elected its chairperson. For the next three years it was her major preoccupation. As I have described earlier, she shepherded it through all the hurdles, right to the end of the 1948 General Assembly meeting in Paris when it was approved by a nearly unanimous vote.

Although I have described her UN experience already in this book, it is impossible to overemphasize the very special relationship Eleanor had with the delegates from other countries. They saw her, of course, as a member of her own U.S. delegation, but also thought of her as objective and genuinely concerned about the human side of the economic and social issues on their agendas, as well as about the future of the smaller member states at the UN. She could even be described as a universal aunt figure—for there were delegates who consulted her on personal matters.

My grandmother continued to serve on the American delegation until John Foster Dulles became secretary of state under President Eisenhower in 1952. Afterward she continued a variety of "good works," principal among them being her untiring support for the American Association for the United Nations.

As she aged she slowed down a bit—but only just a bit—and her schedule until the last year of her life remained very full.

After her husband's death my grandmother had had to put up with the desire of many people to be nostalgic. They plagued her with wanting to know what FDR would have thought or done. She was often asked about the new president. Grandmère had reservations about Mr. Truman, but comparisons were not her way of expressing her criticism. Even my sister and I were often questioned about what our grandfather would have done. Our pat answer was usually, "How should I know?"

My mother and stepfather's reaction to this new situation was courageous, sad, and tragic. Anna and John Boettiger's saga illustrates fully the illusions and delusions of living in the reflected aura of FDR and the first lady, perhaps the most recognized political icons of the twentieth century. Their adjustment brought out the best in my mother, but the worst in my stepfather, who had always been of a depressed nature. It is a story that needs a full narrative telling, and hence it will be described separately in chapter 17.

My sister and I had been well known by many Americans when resident in the White House in our early years. Our identity as "Sistie and Buzzie" was firmly fixed in the public mind during the first half of the 1930s. When we moved to Seattle the spotlight on us markedly diminished. After returning to the White House with our mother, in 1944 and 1945, our shine was only a glimmer. At age fourteen, I was no longer the cute towheaded little darling that I had been at ages three to seven. My Secret Service companionship, meaning with the agents assigned to protect me, was now casual, limited to their accompanying me when I traveled to and from my boarding school.

Both my sister and I had only a modest reaction to no longer being thought of as the president's eldest grandchildren. We had liked our time at the White House—all twelve years of it. It had been exciting, much different than what any of our contemporaries had ever experienced. Yet despite coming to feel "at home" in the White House, we always knew, because we were often reminded, that "we were only visiting."

When my school term ended the June after my grandfather died, I was keenly aware of not heading east to Washington but instead traveling west to Seattle. Without the guiding hand of my assigned bodyguard the Secret Service had assigned—a companionship I'd always had as long as I could remember—I was on my own. I missed the company and was only too aware of how much I depended on those companions to tend to my (our) travel details.

I have attached the rest of my own story to that of my mother and stepfather's.

The president's four sons were given very special recognition—by the public and by the press. It was something my uncles took for granted. It happened wherever they went. They walked into the Copacabana or Toots Shor's and were given the best table. The sturdy men outside the unmarked door of the "21" Club immediately recognized them, and, with nodded acknowledgment, the door swung open.

Here are comments typical of ones I heard as a boy and as a teenager, often from total strangers: I saw your Uncle Jimmy boarding a plane at LaGuardia last week. I heard Elliott on his radio program in Texas. Franklin's wedding to Ethel du Pont was the social event of the year. The newspapers reported that your Uncle John and Aunt Ann were at a dance in Nantucket last week. Just as my mother did, I kept track of her brothers through the press and from the multitude of tales that filtered down to me through my grandmother and mother—one echoing the other.

Often my mother's and grandmother's tones, when passing on such accounts, were meant to be instructive. They were often disapproving when reporting my uncles' scrapes with the press or local authorities, their womanizing, heavy drinking or reckless driving. Or generally calling attention to themselves, showing off. At the same time, both my mother and my grandmother always feel prey to their charms.

Additionally, Eleanor Roosevelt did not approve of her sons' preference for the upper-class types she considered self-centered and indulgent. In my grandmother's view, "society" was a moneyed group of people seemingly unaware of the basic changes rapidly altering America's social landscape. They seemed, she thought, to use their social position to distance themselves from the "hoi polloi," rather than offer any sort of useful stewardship.

By contrast, both my mother and my stepfather—who himself did not come from the social background my uncles belonged to and enjoyed—were very much engaged in the issues my grandmother felt were important. They better understood her beliefs in what mattered, where one's energy should be expended, and thus were approved of fully.

I have recorded how our family was given preferential treatment when visiting the White House, sparking more than a little jealousy and resentment from my uncles and their wives, who found themselves relegated to smaller rooms than even my sister and I had.

Of course it was a completely different scene after FDR died. My grandmother had a new career, a very consuming one as a U.S. delegate to the United Nations. My uncles made the adjustment by changing almost not at all and by continuing to expect the special recognition they were used to.

My mother adjusted to her father's death quite well. To some extent she was still recognized as the daughter of the late president. But I'm afraid that no longer being identified as the president's son-in-law proved too much for John Boettiger to bear.

17

My Mother, the President's Daughter

Our mother told my sister and me very little about her early childhood except what illustrated her own mother's inability to give of herself. Being the eldest child and the only girl—four younger brothers were soon to follow—one might assume that a special relationship would have developed between mother and daughter. However, this was not the case until my mother decided to separate from my own father, many years later. My mother, the eldest, was just a year old when her first brother was born—James—followed thereafter by Elliott, Franklin Jr., and John. My impression is that she was frequently the follower, tagging along—in fact, fairly in awe of her younger brothers. Although not as assertive as they were, she often imitated them, resulting in poor manners that brought them their Grandmother Sara's disapproval.

Our mother did tell Sis and me how she hated the school she was sent to in New York City, Miss Chapin's, a very proper one for upper-class young ladies. "Snobbish" was our mother's condemnation. But she admitted, too, that she had always been in rebellion and never studied.

My grandmother, for her own part, always regretted never having had the opportunity to go to college. So when my mother, Anna, reached that age, Eleanor urged her daughter to do so. Franklin agreed to the idea and suggested the New

York State Agricultural College, hoping his daughter would take an interest in helping to manage the family estate. (On the eight hundred or so acres of the Roosevelt estate there was not only our own family farm but also several tenant farmers. FDR also wished to start up a tree farm). My mother behaved predictably and balked; then a compromise was reached with her agreeing to try college for one semester.

Eleanor Roosevelt drove her daughter down to Schenectady, later recording it as an unpleasant journey. Seemingly, they had exchanged not a word for the entire trip.

Anna's brother Elliot visited her during that semester and reported back that his sister was having a great time—involved with boyfriends and the school dances. Then, upon returning home from her one semester, my mother soon set her sights on getting married. This was quite unlike the untruthful story she told my sister and me about marrying the first eligible man who proposed to her. Anna had many boyfriends, and indeed several suitors, with a busy social life. Her correspondence at the time illustrates this very well. Bent on becoming active in New York's social world, my mother married my father when she was only twenty and, although my father could not afford it, they lived in grand style.

My sister was born in 1927, less than a year after my parents were married. I was born three years later. But soon after my birth, my parents separated.

My first memories of either my father or my mother begin, really, with my mother, sister, and I moving into the White House to live with my grandparents. So with my father, what I recollect is always linked to our visitations with him, my grandmother and my mother having agreed that these should not take place at the White House. Therein begins a saga.

For unclear reasons, my mother—with the support of my grandmother (but not of my great-grandmother, Granny—began to paint a picture of my dad as a "Bad Guy," an undesirable person, describing him as a snob and as prejudicial. This undoubtedly helped justify her choice to separate from him.

When Dad requested a visitation, he would have to take us to New York—as he was blocked from access to Sis and me within the White House. When she would announce Dad's request to us children, my mother's voice and face took on a pained expression, which my sister soon echoed. I didn't! I liked my father and enjoyed my time with him. In response to my positive attitude, my mother would roll her eyes up to the ceiling for my sister's benefit, who then put on an ugly expression. When my sister and I were together (as we usually were for security reasons), her most telling, derisive point to throw at me was, "You're just like Dad!"

It hurt, and I knew I couldn't reply. Sis was only taking on the official attitude toward our father. I couldn't even retort that I *liked* my father, for that would mean contravening the three important ladies in my life, my grandmother, my mother, and my sister. Doing so would have risked my losing all approval from them.

Why my father was vilified—literally made into a "legitimate object of hostility"—I simply do not know. It makes no sense, and the "case" against him is quite inaccurate and even includes outright lies. Most of this, I should add, only came to light when I was doing research for my earlier book at the Roosevelt Library.

So what is a small boy to make of it? It never occurred to me that my mother might be stringing together so many fibs, with my grandmother implicitly backing her. What I didn't know at the time was that our Granny Sara refused to join in the ongoing campaign against Dad. She would invite him to Hyde Park during our New York City visits, and he remained an executor of her estate until her death. Also, when I reviewed my father's correspondence, I found letters to FDR, whose replies were friendly, much like any father-in-law replying cordially to his son-in-law.

During these early years in the White House my mother was often away—she had joined her father's campaign train in the 1932 presidential election and had met a reporter with whom she had fallen in love. My grandmother demonstrated a strong liking for John Boettiger, even though he was a principal reporter for the *Chicago Tribune*, a strongly anti-FDR newspaper. She openly supported his affair with my mother until they were married in 1934–35, at which point I formally acquired a stepfather. My sister, always seeking our mother's approval, immediately showed her affection to this new man in our life.

My own reaction, however, was more reserved. I wondered where this change left my father. My mother never explained. From correspondence between my mother and my grandmother I have since learned that it was expected that my stepfather would become "the man in Buzzie's life." Dad would be further sidelined in their minds. My feelings seemed not to weigh on their thoughts, although it was plainly regretted that I seemed to enjoy my father's company. During our visits with Dad, my sister also seemed to enjoy herself although that was never revealed to our mother.

Then, when Sis and I were respectively eleven and eight (or ten and seven), our nurse who accompanied us on our visit to Plumb Lake with our father, felt moved to write to our mother about my sister's hostile attitude toward Dad. My sister felt she had the license to be rude to Dad, coming very close to being contemptuous. But Sis was simply responding to our mother's continual demonization of him. It was only too clear to me that expressing pleasure in my father's company was too risky. Fearing disapproval, I was caught in a very unhappy situation for a young boy.

My mother's marriage to John Boettiger—now to be called "Uncle J," a label foisted upon me by my mother and sister— encouraged my grandmother to consider us as "The Boettiger Family." This identification was further cemented when they had a child, my half brother Johnny. It was announced to me that Sis now wished to call Uncle J "Popsie."

I have previously, in my book, written of this incident because I was then further pushed into dropping my father's name altogether. Now I was to be known as Curtis Boettiger at school. I surrendered. What else? I would have had to take a stand and I could not bring myself to do that. I was only nine or ten! And I was living in Seattle, three thousand miles away from Dad in New York. I could not manage rebellion. What is more, due to the distance, my father's visits with us were limited. He had to take us with our governess to a fancy hotel resort, an expense he could rarely afford.

When his new wife, Katherine, had a baby, he wrote to my mother to tell her, asking that the news "be conveyed to Sis and Buzz that Katherine had given birth to a little girl," a new half sister for us. Our mother duly informed us but never shared our father's letter with us, nor her very polite response. The net result was that I became more and more Buzz Boettiger, and indeed thought less frequently of my father. To have done otherwise would have meant entering a "no go" area. But still, despite my mother's encouragement, I could not join my sister in her affection for our stepfather. There was indeed no man in my life except my grandfather, and I adored him. And yet for me to say so, implying that I wanted to be like my grandfather, was apparently as close to blasphemy as I could possibly come! In my book I quote my mother's intense reaction, "You can never be like Papa!"

This pattern of watching carefully what I said continued throughout my period of growing up—until I married, in fact—and even then, questions about Dad were never raised with my mother or my sister.

My mother, as they prepared to leave for Seattle, had engineered a post for herself as associate editor of the women's page at the *Post Intelligencer*. Her straining to be a partner with John was her interpretation of the relationship the two of them were meant to have, never one that Popsie himself felt wholly comfortable with. This vision of their life together, however, continued to be what was presented to Sis and me. In later years, my mother admitted to me that within a year or so after John took the job as the newspaper's publisher, she found herself having to spend an inordinate amount of time and energy propping him up. By then it seems he wanted to find a new job, perhaps one closer to being the reporter that he was when he first met my mother. As she put it to me, this constant need to support John—building up his fragile ego—dominated their relationship and continued to do so until 1947, when he was dismissed from our home due to his having had an extramarital affair in Phoenix, Arizona, where they were then living.

During much of the period of my mother's marriage, it was characterized as "made in heaven." And yet it was not the case.

As the years continued in Seattle, there was less mention of my dad—except when he occasionally wanted to make the three-thousand-mile journey to take Sis and me to visit with him for a week. My sister would put up quite a fuss. She wouldn't go, she insisted, but our mother said she had to. Accompanied by a lot of weeping—which I found painful, and would have said so to my mother had I been older—she finally came with me to meet our father. My memory of this last visit before Dad went into the army air force was that my sister found it just as agreeable as I myself did. Still, that was not, of course, the way she recorded it for our mother's ears. I remained in limbo, caught between my affection for my father and risking the disapproval of the all-important women in my life.

I should mention the limited number of friendships my mother and stepfather formed during their six to seven years in Seattle. It boiled down to a few acquaintances but only one real friendship, the Donough family, whose two children were roughly the same age as Sis and me.

My mother and John saw the Donoughs once or twice a week, with my sister and me frequently joining them. Marie Donough was a model wife whose husband, John, had lost a leg in a motorboat accident. Their son, Stanley Jr., was often called upon to assist his father, who continued to love boats. But Marie was his mainstay.

I find it odd that my mother and John did so little socializing, only very occasionally inviting their colleagues from the newspaper to our house for dinner. My mother seemed shy and to find entertaining a daunting task. Her shyness was also fed by her worry that any friendship offered her might be because of "who she was."

Being the president's daughter seemed always to be in the forefront of her mind—my sister and I inherited this inhibition, although to a lesser degree. But it was somewhat paradoxical. For my mother always made sure that people were aware of her relation to FDR. One way or another, too much recognized or too little, she would always complain. For me, "who we were" remained a prominent part of my psyche.

In late 1942 my stepfather, as I have said, made the decision to join the army. It was not a wise one, and it was based on a false assumption, that he would soon be working as an aide to FDR, his father-in-law. By this time my new half brother, Johnny, was three or four years old and quite a handful. As long as she was employed as an associate editor of the *Post Intelligencer*, my mother had a nurse to take care of her youngest son, but following her husband around while he trained for a military government assignment made for a different scenario. Often my mother was on her own full time.

Caring for little Johnny was a new occupation, one for which she was ill prepared, either through inexperience or inclination. She had a rough time but always put on a good front for her mother, which was confirmed by their correspondence. Once John Boettiger was assigned overseas, life was a bit easier. She moved back into the White House, as did Sis and I when we returned home from school for vacations. Plus, help with little Johnny was available from the White House staff. Still, with two children in boarding school and a house in Seattle to find tenants for, she was more than occupied at "keeping the home fires burning."

My mother had tried briefly to keep her position with the Seattle newspaper but soon felt she had to resign. Hence the Boettigers' finances were reduced to an army captain's salary, which meant slim pickings. Although living in the White House was free, any travel across the country was not.

While overseas and disillusioned about not being an aide to the president, nor indeed having any of his newspaper skills exploited, my stepfather began to despair. He expressed relief when promotion to major brought with it access to the senior officers' mess. Nonetheless, my mother still had to step in with letters trying to prop up her husband as best she could. His letters acknowledged that his enlistment had been a foolish idea and had brought upon her immense hardship.

When he returned from overseas service and was assigned a desk job in the Pentagon, my stepfather joined my mother and little Johnny, who were living in the White House. One might have thought that such a change would have raised his spirits, but no. My mother was made to resume her role as cheerleader.

At this point my mother's life suddenly took an interesting turn. Her father asked her to take on, at no salary, chores for him that previously had been carried out by his longtime secretary Missy before she became ill and had to retire. Working, as I've said, from a card table in her bedroom, my mother soon became indispensable to her father.

My mother was also instrumental in securing the medical examinations her father needed. The White House physician chose to belittle Anna's concern for FDR's deteriorating health, but as his daughter, she succeeded in bringing in a heart specialist to attend him. To this day, I believe those activities and responsibilities my mother assumed from the end of 1943 until her father's death, in April 1945, are neither well known nor appropriately evaluated.

The death of Franklin Roosevelt, on April 12, 1945, quickly and drastically altered the world I knew and had come to take for granted. My grandmother, my mother, my stepfather, and kid brother all had to move out of the White House within three days. An apartment at Wardman Park was found for the

Boettigers, John commuting daily to the Pentagon and refusing to give any thought to a postwar career—even though the surrender of Germany was less than a month away. Still they could not reclaim their home on Mercer Island in Seattle until John could be mustered out of the service. He was discharged quickly enough after the German capitulation, and it was to Seattle that I headed home from boarding school the following June.

The letters my mother wrote to me at this time spoke of her worries about the future and the problems facing John with the challenge of new employment. She and I later talked a good deal about that summer of 1945. She and my sister and I were delighted to be home again, but she had been right: our stepfather was depressed. He pottered around the house doing odd jobs, but could not focus on new career possibilities. It was my mother who did this by continuing to raise opportunities to be explored. My stepfather was dismissive of everything, and she warned me to be very careful of what I said to him. His fragility was apparent. My mother had to "walk on eggshells," she reported.

When Sis and I left to go back to school, nothing had seriously been explored for John's future. He had found fault with every possibility in spite of, or possibly because of, my mother's greater objectivity. In fact I feel he may have resented her "pushing" him. Perhaps because he felt all the tension in the air, little brother Johnny was extraordinarily cranky and disagreeable. Sis and I agreed that "it was not a summer to be remembered." If she had been privy to our view, our mother would probably have agreed.

Throughout the rest of 1945, and well into 1946, talk continued about what to do, with my stepfather continuing to be generally negative about any option. Finally a decision was made that they would start up a liberal newspaper in the American Southwest, in Phoenix, Arizona. At the time I assumed that my stepfather, with his experience as a publisher, and my mother, who was perhaps more ideological but always sensible, would have thought through this enterprise, especially the finances. First a weekly, then a biweekly, next three times a week, and finally a daily, the *Arizona Times* emerged before Christmas of 1946—eating up prodigious amounts of money all the way.

As I later learned, John Boettiger's planning had been less than competent. Fundraising now consumed much of my mother's time, with the pitch most often trading on the memory of Franklin Roosevelt. My mother was remarkably successful in repeatedly refinancing the *Arizona Times* but, having been an unrealistic pipe dream from the start, it was finally closed in the summer of 1948, with my mother selling the presses and the premises for a pittance.

My stepfather, following an extramarital affair departed from the household. First, however, he had managed to spend the rest of what was left of the Boettiger family's capital, leaving my mother quite penniless.

We saw my sister married in June of that year, and I moved to Los Angeles where I had the promise of a summer job. My mother later moved there as well to edit a women's magazine and to broadcast a radio show with her celebrated mother, Eleanor Roosevelt. She now had to depend on that mother to supplement her income.

I have great admiration for my mother's coping with this difficult time in her life. Her "made in heaven" marriage had blown apart and she had had to assume responsibilities well beyond her experience. What rose to the surface was her fortitude and integrity. It was a turning point in her life. For the first time she was alone, really alone, really on her own. Sis was married, and I was gone to college, though close to home. We had an apartment on the second floor of a duplex house in a nondescript area south of Hollywood. She had the radio program with her mother and her editorial job to occupy her. The income from these, unfortunately, did not enable a lifestyle anywhere close to what she had enjoyed in Seattle. Still, we had a cook-housekeeper. Mother was at home most evenings and kept up "standards" with supper served us by our cook. My kid brother—now nine years old—had been fed earlier, and after a day of school was ready for bed. My mother and I talked openly; it was then that I was "filled in" on her life with John Boettiger, who would appear occasionally to take young Johnny off for a day or two.

As in Seattle, my mother made only a few friends in Los Angeles and I often tagged along at the weekend. But she did not appear to be lonely. In retrospect I do wonder that she wasn't so, with her father dead, her mother three thousand miles away, and with no longer any man in her life. I was her only steady companion. Usually we had a drink together before supper. I would make her a martini and open a beer for myself.

My mother and I talked together easily. We both followed the political events of the day. For her this was not just routine, but now essential, background for her radio program with Eleanor. Now eighteen, I had just returned from spending three months in Paris with my grandmother, who had been attending the United Nations Regular Assembly where she was one of the senior U.S. delegates.

What was too bad was that the thirteen weeks of network funding for the radio program collapsed when no sponsor was found. To make matters worse, my mother became ill with what was finally diagnosed as "desert fever." I wonder if the doctors didn't make this up for lack of a more precise diagnosis. My guess is that she just collapsed from the strain of the past three years of such stress and responsibilities, and, moreover, found herself depressed with nothing specific to look forward to in the future. She had to accept $100 a month from her mother to help out financially.

Finally, my mother moved to San Francisco for medical reasons, leaving me alone with the housekeeper and Johnny, who had recently been placed in boarding school. I got along fine with my 1939 Chevrolet to scoot me about the vast spaces of Los Angeles. I had a girlfriend and often stayed for supper with her family. My meager allowance sufficed as it covered the cost of gasoline and the occasional movie. My girlfriend's parents were very understanding about my "short rations" and fed me regularly.

Soon my mother's medical treatments were extended, and she moved Johnny to San Francisco to be with her. I soon decided to give up college and go to work in New York—and also to get married at the tender age of twenty. This did mean that my mother could reduce expenses and stop having to keep up a home for me in L.A.

As a consequence I know little about her life in San Francisco or her subsequent move back to Los Angeles, where she met and married her third husband, a physician, James Halsted. Jim had three children at home, all teenagers, so my mother was once again fully occupied with these three plus Johnny.

With me three thousand miles away in New York, I only saw my mother occasionally over the next several years. Jim was restless as chief medical officer at various VA hospitals and kept my mother moving house. In Syracuse my mother successfully reestablished herself as an editor, only to find that Jim then intended to take a Fulbright Scholarship and spend three years in a hospital in Shiraz, Iran. Her new career went up in smoke. After stints in Kentucky and Michigan, she wound up in Washington DC, where Jim was working in the headquarters of the Department of Veterans Affairs. There was no job for his wife, Anna, but she became involved in a multiplicity of volunteer commitments, including the Washington Work and Training Opportunity Center, Americans for Democratic Action, the Capitol Area Division of the United Nations Association of the United States of America, the National Committee of Household Employment, the Wiltwyck School, and the Eleanor Roosevelt Foundation.

When Jim reached retirement age, my mother having inherited money in her father's will, acquired a property in Hillsdale, New York, about a half-hour drive from Hyde Park and Val-Kill. Were those retirement years at Hillsdale ones of contentment? I don't know. Certainly when I visited they seemed to be. But then my mother had long been good at putting on a good front.

In 1975 she became very ill with throat cancer, dying in early December in Mount Sinai Hospital in New York City. She is buried in the family plot at St. James Church Cemetery in Hyde Park.

Since her death I have thought a good deal about my legacy from her. It is a decidedly mixed bag. What did I pick up from my mother? What traits, viewpoints, tastes, and habits do I have that I can trace back to her? Or think that I can?

Number one would be perseverance, especially the capacity to "put up with things," which includes "making do." But that doesn't mean I'm unwilling to experiment.

Although my mother was not above lying (as she regularly did to my father), she possessed a basic integrity that I really saw plainly when she was left on her own with the *Arizona Times* and was forced to wind down that organization—a responsibility that left her without funds. It sounds rather old-fashioned, but my mother was a very decent person. It reflected her values.

I tilt on my mother being uncomfortable with, really unable to tolerate, criticism. She couldn't abide it. I inherited that, but not, I think, as intensely as she was afflicted. As a child, finding my way around my mother took some ingenuity— and I became quite adept. But it was always a challenge.

My resentment when it comes to being corrected is about average, I feel. But criticism is another thing. There I am unduly sensitive.

Curtis Roosevelt

APRIL 19, 1930–SEPTEMBER 26, 2016

We are thankful he lived long enough to complete this book but at the same time very sad he will not be able to see its publication.

2. Hyde Park, Our Family Home

1. Beebee, my nurse, being African American, was most unusual in our upper-class circle.

2. The breaststroke, the backstroke, and the sidestroke were considered, I was informed, most appropriate for ladies.

3. David McCullough writes about Sara Delano Roosevelt in *Psychology Today*, March 1983, 36: "She had standards, and she had the gift for making everybody want to measure up."

4. Geoffrey Ward, *A First-Class Temperament: The Emergence of Franklin Roosevelt* (New York: Harper and Row, 1989), 48.

3. FDR and Eleanor Roosevelt

All quotations by Eleanor Roosevelt in this chapter are from *The Autobiography of Eleanor Roosevelt* (New York: Harper Perennial, reprint edition, October 21, 2014).

1. A book review by Seamus Perry in the *Literary Review* of December 2012 describes it: "the very idea of a Victorian, possessing the full mixture of suppressed turmoil, self blindness, and strenuous achievement."

2. See chapter 9 in this book on Eleanor Roosevelt's "taking against" her mother-in-law.

3. For a fuller picture of this incident, I refer the reader to Geoffrey Ward's book *A First-Class Temperament*.

4. Lash's account is what Eleanor Roosevelt told him, hence not altogether reliable. Many of her stories to Joe—and often to the rest of us just sitting around after supper at Val-Kill—were much embroidered. Only by reading the relevant correspondence, as I had to do when writing my book, does one clearly see this. See Joseph P. Lash's biography *Eleanor and Frank-*

lin: The Story of Their Relationship, Based on Eleanor Roosevelt's Private Papers (New York: W. W. Norton, 2014). First published 1971.

5. Letter from Dr. Lawrence Kubie to Joseph Lash, June 7, 1964 in the Franklin Delano Roosevelt Library archives.

6. Ward, *First-Class Temperament,* 676–77.

7. Marion Dickerman's autobiography emphasizes the rapport she had with FDR.

8. Jim Farley was the chair of the Democratic National Committee.

6. Eleanor's Book on Etiquette

1. See my book *Too Close to the Sun* (New York: PublicAffairs, 2008), 109–11.

2. See chapter 4, "White House Pleasures of the Table," in this volume.

3. According to a recent biography of Emily Post, we learn that she had a social conscience and would probably have shared Eleanor Roosevelt's concern for people to feel comfortable in social situations. See Laura Claridge's *Emily Post* (New York: Random House, 2008).

9. Eleanor and Her Mother-in-Law

1. Eleanor went to live with her Grandmother Hall after both her parents had died.

2. Jan Pottker, *Sara and Eleanor: The Story of Sara Delano Roosevelt and Her Daughter-in-Law, Eleanor Roosevelt* (New York: St. Martin's Press, 2014), 121.

3. See Jan Pottker's *Sara and Eleanor,* 125–26.

4. Pottker, *Sara and Eleanor,* 142.

5. Joseph P. Lash in his authorized biography, *Eleanor and Franklin.*

6. Ward, *First-Class Temperament,* chapter 7.

7. Pottker, *Sara and Eleanor,* 191.

8. Eleanor recognized this personal limitation even with her friends. She writes to Lorena Hickok: "Yes, dear, you are right. I give everyone the feeling that you have that I have 'taken them on' & don't need anything from them & then when they naturally resent it & don't like to accept it from me, I wonder why! It is funny I know & I can't help it *something locked me up & I can't unlock!*" My italics. Quoted in Joseph Lash's *Love, Eleanor: Eleanor Roosevelt and Her Friends, 1943–1963* (New York: Doubleday, 1982), 201, published twenty years after my grandmother died.

9. Most of these references to Sara's engagements with social organizations are drawn from Jan Pottker's *Sara and Eleanor.*

10. Joseph Lash, *Eleanor and Franklin,* 293.

11. Lash, *Eleanor and Franklin,* 329.

12. Lash, *Eleanor and Franklin,* 329–30.

13. Lash, *Love, Eleanor,* 56–57.

14. Doris Kearns Goodwin, *No Ordinary Time* (New York: Simon and Schuster, 1994).

15. Quote from Bernard Asbell, *Mother and Daughter: The Letters of Eleanor and Anna Roosevelt* (New York: Fromm International, 1988).

10. Others in the White House

1. Taken from a quote in Jean Edward Smith's book *FDR* (New York: Random House, 2007).

11. The Chaste Eleanor Roosevelt

1. Lash, *Love, Eleanor*, 205.

2. Eleanor Roosevelt, *If You Ask Me* (New York: Appleton-Century, 1946), 93.

3. I write about this in my book *Too Close to the Sun*.

13. To Europe with My Grandmother

1. Dulles was one of the senior U.S. delegates in Paris as it was expected that Thomas E. Dewey would be elected president in 1948 and Dulles would be his secretary of state. (That Truman beat Dewey was a real shock.)

2. Joseph Lash, *Eleanor: The Years Alone* (New York: W. W. Norton, 1972), 157. Unfortunately the author doesn't relate how seriously religious my grandmother actually was.

3. All the quotes in this section are taken from Mary Ann Glendon, *A World Made New: Eleanor Roosevelt and the Universal Declaration of Human Rights* (New York: Random House, 2001).

4. He was of the minority sect, Ahmadiyya Muslim. Later he was appointed a justice of the World Court. Shortly after I joined the UN Secretariat he popped into my office one day to give me a copy of the Koran—which he had translated into English!

14. Roosevelt as Commander in Chief

1. Eric Larrabee, *Commander in Chief: Franklin Delano Roosevelt, His Lieutenants, and Their War* (New York: Simon and Schuster, 1988), 642.

2. Larrabee, *Commander in Chief*, 638.

15. Roosevelt and Winston Churchill

1. Roy Jenkins, *Churchill: A Biography* (New York: Plume, 2001), 785.

2. Churchill had held cabinet posts during World War I and after, as well as in the early 1920s. Roosevelt had been assistant secretary of the navy for eight years during President Wilson's administration, 1912–20.

3. David Dilks, ed., *The Diaries of Sir Alexander Cadogan, OM, 1938–1945* (London: Faber and Faber, 2010).

4. Likewise, the title of Geoffrey Ward's second volume on FDR was taken from Oliver Wendell Holmes's comment about FDR when he was campaigning for the presidency in 1932: "a second-class intellect but a first-class temperament."

5. The U.S. Army Chief of Staff General George C. Marshall took this stance throughout the war. He was the only close aid of FDR's who was not called by his first name.

6. Note the Tolstoy Conference in Moscow in October 1944.

7. Dilks, ed., *Diaries of Sir Alexander Cadogan*.

8. Lady Soames, Churchill's last surviving child, made plain to me her father's hurt feelings over lunch one day at the Reform Club. Later, after my talk at the Churchill Museum in London, she wrote me a nice note telling me that she was grateful to see that a Roosevelt family member fully acknowledged the awkward situation between her father and my grandfather during the Yalta Conference.